What Development Is All About

CHINA·INDONESIA·BANGLADESH

For Kumu
whose brief appearance
in this book on page 144
is really the heart
of the story.

Books by Douglas Roche, M.P.

The Catholic Revolution, 1968.
Man to Man, 1969.
It's A New World, 1970.
Justice, Not Charity: A New Global Ethic for Canada, 1976.
The Human Side of Politics, 1976.

What Development Is All About

CHINA·INDONESIA·BANGLADESH

by Douglas Roche M.P.

NC Press Limited
Toronto, 1979

Canadian Cataloguing in Publication Data
Main entry under title:
What Development is All About.

ISBN 0–919601–44–8

1. China — Economic conditions — 1949–
2. Asia — Economic conditions — 1945–
3. Economic assistance, Canadian — Asia.   I Title.

HC427.9.R63   330.9′51′05   C79–094603–3

We would like to thank the Ontario Arts Council and the Canada Council for their assistance in the production of this book.

New Canada Publications, a division of NC Press Limited, Box 4010, Station A, Toronto, Ontario, M5W 1H8. (416) 368-1165.

Contents

Foreword

Douglas Roche in this book says many things about human development, about foreign aid and about three Asian countries (Bangladesh, China, and Indonesia) which would be open to radically different interpretations. It is impossible to write of the deep and disturbing questions of economic justice which face humanity today without being controversial.

A major portion of the manuscript deals with China's development experience. In some circles debunking China is fashionable today. The Chinese themselves are partly responsible for this. Many things which were said and believed in the past have now been rejected in Beijing (Peking) itself.

Roche's book is timely, however, because it looks at problems which go deeper than the study of minutiae by China watchers. Roche writes not as a China expert but as a specialist in Third World development. From this perspective the struggles of intra-Party politics in Beijing pale in light of the vast difference between China (whether now, or three years ago, or a decade ago) and development in Indonesia, Bangladesh, and almost all other Third World countries.

As Roche shows, the basic difference is that China has taken seriously the problem of people at the local community level. Emphasis was put on human values to create a social base on which higher technological advances could be made. The current Chinese desire to absorb Western technology is in line with the long-range goals set out by Mao Zedong and Zhou Enlai long ago, however surprising other changes may be.

The question Roche raises is whether there is hope for genuine development in other parts of the Third World. Canadian government and non-government efforts to help in the progress of people are often bogged down in inappropriate technology. As the author suggests, with government aid this is the result of considering the foreign trade advantages for Canada rather than the real needs of the recipients.

In his sober but not despairing account, Roche shows his own human sensitivity and concern. Again and again, real people flash on the mind as Roche recounts illuminating detail or revealing anecdote. Experienced Asia travellers will find memories flooding back; those who have never been to Asia will find vivid descriptions of Asians in many contexts.

This book is not the last word on China or the Third World or foreign aid. It argues forcefully on the question of values and human development, however, and offers useful insights on how freedom, religion, and commitment relate to this question.

The following church organizations have co-operated in supporting this publication:

Canada China Programme of the Canadian Council of Churches

Canadian Catholic Organization for Development and Peace

Primate's World Development and Relief Fund of the Anglican Church

Scarboro Foreign Mission Society

Ten Days for World Development

United Church Division of Communication

United Church Division of World Outreach.

This support while not indicating agreement on all points, means that the book is recommended for study by church and community groups. Suggestions on further resources for study groups can be found at the end of the book.

Study of Douglas Roche's book by individuals and groups will reward readers with a clear comparative analysis, and well-written descriptions of people and situations in Asia which impinge on the lives of us all. Such study will open new perspectives and force us to a great deal of rethinking on what human development is all about.

	Raymond L. Whitehead, Director,
Toronto, Canada,	*Canada China Programme,*
July 1979.	*Canadian Council of Churches.*

Introduction
The Costs and Benefits of Human Development

This is a book about human development. Not the whole vast spectrum of humanity. Rather, it is the account of a six-week journey in Asia where I examined the model of development in China and contrasted it with an entirely different model in Indonesia and Bangladesh. What I saw convinced me that Canada's foreign aid program, administered by the Canadian International Development Agency (CIDA), must be over-hauled if we are serious about actually helping to make self-reliant, dignified human beings out of the world's poverty-stricken millions.

There is a growing number of Canadians skeptical of foreign aid and even hostile to the Third World as revealed in a letter from Stewart MacArthur of Toronto, to the editor of the *Toronto Star*, published the day I left Canada on my journey: "(The Government has) squandered our foreign aid, pouring money down the bottomless rat holes of starving countries that refuse to curb their population growth."

Since Canada's foreign aid in 1979–80 is $1.21 billion (approximately 2% of the federal budget and .45% of our Gross National Product), the government cannot ignore the opinion of the Stewart MacArthurs of Canada. It is much more useful, however, to ask deeper questions concerning the changing relationship of Canada to the developing nations. In fact, the time has come when those who feel warmest toward the Third World should probe the faults and failures of policies in both the developed and developing nations.

Why has a quarter-century of foreign aid poured into the Third World countries not closed the rich-poor gap? Who is the chief beneficiary of aid? Why is China, the largest country in the world with 850 million people, making great gains in development without any outside help at all? To ask these questions is to plunge beneath the superficialities and hypocrisy of much that passes for "international assistance" and to begin to distinguish between foreign aid and human development. They are by no means the same thing — as China bears witness.

No one interested in the complex problems of economic and social development in the modern world can ignore what is happening in China today. The People's Republic of China, formed when the Communist Party of Mao Zedong (Mao Tse-tung*) took power in 1949, has become a highly regimented, controlled, collectivist state, determined to be self-reliant and independent of foreign interference and influence. In the view of some development experts, the Chinese experiment may well be the greatest the world has ever known. For China is reputed to provide a basic level of food, shelter, health services, education and work for all its inhabitants. If China can become self-reliant, why can't the poverty-stricken Third World countries achieve this also? What lessons can the developing countries learn from China?

At the invitation of the Chinese People's Institute of Foreign Affairs, I spent eighteen days examining China's food production related to population pressures, industrialization programs in smaller centres, innovations in agricultural and industrial development, and the process of economic planning.

For my companions I selected Bernard Wood and Clyde Sanger, two experts on development with whom I have worked in Ottawa. Wood is director of the North-South Institute, a private body set up to extend research and public communication on the development questions. Sanger, a first-rate journalist, was then an information officer for the Ottawa-based International Development Research Centre. I explained to the Chinese that my wife Eva is director of Early Childhood Development, a teacher-training program at Grant MacEwen Community College in Edmonton, and wanted to study day care facilities for children in China. They agreed to set up a special program for her.

We entered China through Hong Kong, travelling by train to Guangzhou (Canton) and by air to Beijing (Peking) where my study began with a two-hour interview with Miss Wang Hairong, Vice-Minister of Foreign Affairs and a niece of Chairman Mao. Following three days in Beijing, we travelled to Yan-Chuan and Hsi-Yang to visit the Dazhai (Tachai) Brigade model agricultural community, Shijiazhuang, Anyang, and Linxian (Linhsien) to study the economic effects of the Red Flag Canal's irrigation and electrification system, Zhengzhou, Nanjing (Nanking), Wuxi, Shanghai, Zhong Hua County, and Guangzhou. We travelled 4 000 km. by air, 3 000 km. by train and 1 800 km. by car inside China, visiting communes, production brigades, factories, power stations, housing complexes, schools, nurseries, health stations, Chinese in their homes, and several cultural performances. Often we took the opportunity to walk through the streets.

Though planned long beforehand, the trip occurred two

Since my visit, China has adopted the Pinyin alphabet. I have changed the spelling of Chinese names accordingly from the former Wade-Giles system.

months after the death of Mao on September 9, 1976; the Chinese leadership was still sorting out the legacy of the Chairman's accomplishments and the problems of party disunity, economic dislocation and labour discontent. No land having been so insulated, so little understood from outside and so caricatured, China from afar seems an island of stability. But it was clear that underneath the tranquility there was considerable turmoil.

In fact, the day we left China, the Hong Kong newspapers reported that the Chinese army had been called in to put down uprisings in four provinces. Since then, there has been one shock wave after another, the speed of China's modernization program startling even experienced China-watchers. That China would normalize relations with the U.S., sign a trade treaty with Japan, and tolerate mass rallies around Beijing's "Democracy Wall" within two years of our visit would not have seemed possible. Yet all this, and much more, has happened as China accelerates the Four Modernizations — development of agriculture, industry, science and technology and national defence to the level of an industrialized nation by the year 2000.

In the Afterword, I will discuss some of the implications of this burst of pragmatism in relation to the theme of this book: human development. At this point I caution the reader not to expect a full interpretation of all the changes in China. The book, which is in the main a journal of my findings, is set in a specific time frame. It is still too early to tell if the apparent egalitarian features of Chinese socialism will be helped or hindered by the rapid infusion of Western technology. What is important to understand at this moment of transition is that China has a base of human development on which to overlay modernization. Most developing countries have tried to modernize without laying such a base.

As one who has travelled through Third World countries for many years, it was a lesson to me to see how the Chinese people have made themselves self-reliant. I do not hold that China is *the* model of development. I am sure it would be possible to find deprivation among China's vast and far-flung population. Yet there is a movement toward continually advancing the common good. That movement is based on a massive populist motivation I have not seen elsewhere.

Is it necessary to infuse a populace with Maoist philosophy in order to motivate people to take development into their own hands and march by the thousands, pick and shovel in hand, to the site of a canal or dam construction?

That is a question I struggled with as I continued my journey through Indonesia and Bangladesh. I chose those two countries because they are huge, quite different Asian societies and are among the top ten recipients of aid from Canada. Indonesia's 135.2 million population (fifth largest country in the world) and Bangladesh's 80.4 million (eighth largest) make these nations a vital part of Asia, a continent containing three-fifths of all teen-agers and children in the world.

It is clear that Indonesia and Bangladesh do not have the egalatarian motivation that characterizes development in China. Despite their political liberation from the big powers, the two countries are ruled by people who still think in terms of economic elitism. It was a shock for me to come out of China, where rural development is so pronounced, into Indonesia and Bangladesh where rural development is so pitiful. Though 81% of Indonesians and 93% of Bengalis live in the rural areas, the fruits of whatever development there has been in these two countries have gone to the upper strata, while the lower strata has not seen much improvement. Can we say development has taken place in the face of a terrible shortage of health, education, and housing services?

In the West we have been conditioned to think that a transfer of technology, through foreign aid, will produce developed societies in the poor nations. China destroys that myth. On the eve of the United Nations Third Development Decade, starting in 1980, we ought to have learned by now that true human development the world over requires changing economic and social systems to allow for more equitable sharing of global resources in a spirit of stewardship and social justice.

In the history of the world, the usual route to social gains has been through revolution and violence. China herself is a case in point. I do not rule out the possibility of more waves of violence by people who are economically discriminated against. But for the safety of the world in the nuclear age, as well as for social justice, it makes political sense to concentrate our attention and action on enlightened international partnerships that will promote an even level of human development.

Development, in its fullest sense, means liberation of the human spirit made possible by securing an essential economic base. True development does not pit the spirit of man against economic progress in some kind of contest. Rather it encompasses the wholeness of man and promotes the economic, social and cultural well-being of the individual. In the end, development is an ethical question because human dignity — which is the goal of development — can only be measured by quality of life standards, not just quantity of life.

Neither the model of development in China nor the model in

Indonesia and Bangladesh is satisfactory. But we will not be able to find the right model unless we understand, in human terms, the costs and benefits of each.

Acknowledgments

My travel companions in China, Bernard Wood, Clyde Sanger and my wife Eva, not only made my journey more pleasant but added valuable impressions in long taping sessions. Congenial though we were our judgments differed on several occasions, as the reader will observe. The same can be said of Ray Verge, my companion in Indonesia and Bangladesh, who is pioneering the Alberta Government's aid program.

My trip to China resulted from an invitation by the former Chinese Ambassador to Canada, Zhang Wenjin, on behalf of the People's Institute of Foreign Affairs. All the Chinese officials I met were unfailingly courteous and anxious that I learn as much as possible (in what they hoped would be only my first visit) about their country. In all the Asian countries I visited, the External Affairs and Canadian International Development Agency (CIDA) officers of the Canadian government provided a much-appreciated professional service.

As usual, the Parliamentary Librarian, Erik Spicer, and Chief of Parliamentary Research, Philip Laundy, and their staffs, made enormous amounts of material available to me. Bob Miller, of the Parliamentary Centre for Foreign Affairs, provided valuable criticism of the manuscript.

I am indebted to the Rev. R. C. Plant, Associate Secretary, Division of Communications, United Church of Canada, and Raymond L. Whitehead, Director of the Canada-China Programme of the Canadian Council of Churches, for the deep interest they took in this project and the latter for the preface he so kindly contributed. A number of their associates, including such experienced Sinophiles as Don Willmott and Katherine Hockin, read the manuscript, which reassured me without relieving me of my own responsibility.

My research assistant, Gail Paine, and my secretaries, Pamela Miles-Seguin and Betty Mitchell, provided the kind of assistance I have come to depend on.

Finally my literary agent, Ruth Fraser, gave me the encouragement and guidance necessary to see the project through and I am especially grateful to her.

Douglas Roche, M.P.,
Edmonton,
June 25, 1979.

PART I

China: Equality

November 15:
To Learn, To Struggle, To Do

The first thing I noticed about Madame Sung Liying was her rough, calloused hands and a missing finger. She is 46, the mother of four children, and vice chairman in charge of women's affairs at the famous Dazhai (Tachai) Brigade in eastern Shanxi Province. Her eyes and the lines on her face, as well as her hands, bespeak a life of hard work. "We never saw this kind of food before Liberation," she said, looking at the scrambled eggs, meats, peanuts and plum jam on the guest house breakfast table. Madame Sung escorted us through the terraces and gullies of Dazhai, and it was clear that when she spoke of the back-breaking work of building terraces and fields on steep, uncultivated slopes, she did so from experience.

The history of Dazhai and its heroic accomplishments made it for some years before the latest modernization period a model for the new China. In the feudal period before the Mao era, one landlord and three managers controlled most of the land in the Dazhai area, which had little value because the tiny plots teetering on the slopes could not retain water, earth or fertilizer after any sizable rain. Extortion appropriated most of the product of the peasants' labours.

After Liberation the land was put under collective ownership and the people formed a cooperative. Formerly barren land became productive when irrigation was introduced and erosion controlled. The villagers even made their own tools and drilling rods to quarry stone for embankments. When floods in the early 1960's swept away their work they built stronger walls to shore up the tiers of terraces.

The village-sized Brigade, beginning to see their own strength and benefitting from increased yields, grew bolder. In 1970 they began to lop off hilltops and fill in gullies. Hills began to bloom with grapevines; apple, pear and date trees began to appear. Neat rows of new houses were built. Farm mechanization is now progressing as well as forestry, animal husbandry and fish farming. An atmosphere of energy and optimism prevails, which Madame Sung seemed anxious for us to absorb.

In fact it was a speech by Hua Guofeng — entitled "Let the whole party mobilize for a vast effort to develop agriculture, and build Dazhai-type counties throughout the country" — made nearly a year before he succeeded Mao as chairman that helped Hua to the top. It was the speech of a no-nonsense manager, saying that some county officials were "soft, lax and lazy," and ought to develop the spirit of Dazhai.

In 1964 Mao had praised the heroism of the people of Dazhai in overcoming floods that swept away their homes and in rebuilding their land in terraces. In agriculture, learn from Dazhai, he told the rest of China. Hua took this argument a step further by pointing out that the 200 000 people of Xiyang County (which includes Dazhai) had indeed learned from its model, and if all the counties of Shanxi Province did as well as Xiyang, the amount of marketable grain there could increase fourfold. So the pressure is on to bring other counties to the level of Xiyang, or a Dazhai-type, county. In 1975, by Hua's calculation, there were already 300 that qualified and the goal is now 100 new Dazhai-type counties a year for the next five years.

There were so many visitors to Dazhai that accommodation was a problem. Our local host, Wang Paijen, a short, alert man waiting on the platform with four army-type parkas for us, apologized that 100 Japanese had suddenly filled up all the space and we would have to stay at a hotel five kilometres away.

The sight of women pounding rocks and children carrying pails of earth on shoulder poles became common as we walked through Dazhai. I cringed when I first saw women and children at physical labour. This is foreign to my values. And yet throughout the day I felt that a sense of normalcy and even happiness was present in these group efforts.

The levelling of hills seems to be a never-ending job, as does brick-making and the grinding of maize. I do not think the work projects we saw in operation were put on for our benefit, though the workers' dwellings we were taken to were surely models kept ready for visitors.

The apartment blocks are built into the side of a hill for insulation. We saw several two-room units. In one of them, a grand-mother was caring for a small child. This family has a total of seven persons who sleep on two large platform beds kept warm by a coal fire directly underneath.

There was a small kitchen with utensils hanging on the wall, but no running water; there are communal toilets. The dwelling was much too neat, considering that seven people live in such a small area. Food was stored in jars and clothes in trunks. A big picture of Chairman Mao dominated the front room. Wicker chairs, a radio and a sewing machine were the main items of furniture. Outside, cabbages and cornflower were drying in the sunlight. As we left to go to lunch, 150 children had been assembled in a courtyard to applaud us and sing some songs. Every one of them had fat cheeks and was warmly dressed.

I thought the banquet prepared for us was over-doing the welcome. At first the assortment of cold meats seemed just right for an adequate meal, but that, of course, was only the beginning. A whole fish done in a sauce, dumplings filled with pork and very fine egg rolls, turkey and lotus seeds followed. Our Chinese hosts were in an exhuberant mood as they recounted how Dazhai was influencing the rest of China. When it came to toasts, Eva proposed one to the women of China. Madame Sung immediately escalated this to "The women of the world."

We toured a nitrogen fertilizer plant, shown to us as an example of the light industry spawned by the Dazhai development. Using low-grade coal, mined locally, the plant seemed almost improvised as it turned out mounds of fertilizer that would later be mixed with sheep dung and "night soil." The 450 workers, including 80 women, were split into three shifts for continuous production. There are eight grades of pay (the lowest about $9 a month) without a significant variation from bottom to top.

Traditional fertilization practices in China are based on a careful recycling of organic matter. Chemical fertilizers, chiefly ammonium bicarbonate, are now being produced in many small plants throughout China. The target of 3% growth in agricultural yield per year led to the decision to purchase from the United States and other nations 13 large ammonium plants and 13 matching plants for making urea. The combination of importing large-scale fertilizer plants with their enriched capacity of nutrients and the domestic program of building more small plants, such as the one at Dazhai, indicates that China's growth of foodgrains production may be maintained. Premier Allan Blakeney of Saskatchewan had been to Dazhai recently trying to sell his province's potash.

As we walked along, Eva and I talked to the two young

women learning English at Beijing University who had joined us to practise. One of them, Miss An-lsia, told us she had worked in the fields for four years after finishing high school before being selected for language training.

"Would you like to travel or study abroad now that you know English?" Eva asked.

"I will work at whatever I am assigned to do," Miss Du replied, but the sparkle in her eye suggested a will of her own.

At the Dazhai Museum, filled with model displays of before-and-after Liberation, a series of girls gave the opening explanation in each area in reasonably good English. But when we asked questions, they were unable to comprehend or speak extemporaneously. They had been studying English for only three months, we were told.

The exhibit made clear the three rules of Dazhai: 1. Never be self-serving; 2. Never take any privileges; 3. Take an active part in work. To these rules, Hong, our responsible person, added his own trilogy to characterize the success of the Dazhai spirit: 1. To learn; 2. To struggle; 3. To do.

Hard work for the revolutionary cause is certainly more than a slogan here. Without adding new land, without any outside assistance, a basic group of about 150 able-bodied people have transformed the adversities of nature into bountiful harvests. They not only gather enough maize, sorghum and wheat for themselves, a considerable surplus is sold to the state. Dazhai leaders estimate that each member of the Brigade produces about a tonne of grain each year. Moreover, a 10 h.p. tractor designed at Dazhai for their special needs — one with a tight turning circle and caterpillar tracks for climbing slopes — is now being produced in other centres for equally difficult terrains.

"You can't help but be impressed at the fantastic work that has gone into bringing those gullies under cultivation and the overall trebling of yields," Clyde observed.

Bernie felt we were seeing the pragmatic integration of ideology and practicality. "Against a dreadful background of underdevelopment and misery, people now realize that by a team effort and mutual support they are guaranteed minimum benefits. People seem to feel that it is in their interest to be part of the group and to pitch in. There are sacrifices but also benefits."

There are, in fact, similarities between the communal life of Dazhai and monastic living: common manual work for the good of the community; a sense of restraint and sharing; a willingness to engage in self-criticism. Which raises the question: are the people selfless or essentially pragmatic? Having provided themselves with a basic existence, will they, and their children, not want more material goods as time passes? Is it realistic to think that the Chinese will not be like everyone else and demand more consumer goods as the reward for their higher production? In other words, maybe it's premature, after only two generations, to celebrate the Chinese experiment as a new model for human society.

The New China has captured the imagination of many Western observers who despair at the ceaseless cycle of greed that props up industrial society. But technology has a momentum of its own and China, like every other rapidly modernizing country, will have to cope with it. Puzzling as they are, some of the aspects of the Chinese model are very attractive — and they make you think about the future of mankind.

November 16:
"Seeing Is Believing"

It has taken a few days to focus our trip on what we came to see —
development. Yesterday at Dazhai was the first opportunity we had
to see a good example of how people have transformed their own
lives. We emphasized several times to Hong that we wanted to concentrate on food production related to population pressures; industrialization programs in the rural areas; the willingness of the people to accept restraint; appropriate technology at the local level;
the process of economic planning. After all, a central goal of modern China is to be a major socialist industrial power by the year
2000.

Yet the Chinese apparently consider it unthinkable for a visitor not to see the Imperial Palaces, the Ming Tombs, and the Great
Wall, so our first stop in Beijing was the Forbidden City, a great
complex of palaces that for centuries housed a succession of feudal
emperors. The priceless works of art, the ivories, jades, porcelains
and jeweled treasures of the Ming and Ching dynasties are on display but, of course, the real message to the viewer is political: these
emperors built fantastic tributes to themselves on the backs of the
impoverished and oppressed peasants.

The extravagance of the palaces and apartments constructed
for assorted empresses and imperial concubines stunned us. We
drifted through the Hall of Supreme Harmony, the Hall of Preserv-
ing Harmony, the Palace of Earthly Tranquility, the Palace of
Heavenly Purity, the Palace of Gathering Excellence — until I
wanted to scream "Stop! You've made your point." But instead I
tuned out the celestial firmament of the emperors and gazed on the
people of today.

A most astonishing thing was that we ourselves became the objects of attention. Crowds of Chinese tourists circled us as we moved through the palaces, gaping at us as if these strange Western faces were some new *objet d'art*. Most men and women wore rough, blue jackets and trousers, very clean and warm looking. The men had close-cropped hair. The local guide, a young woman, had no compunction about ordering people aside so we could pass. I was a little uncomfortable at this but only smiled weakly at the people.

The Ming Tombs, about an hour north of Beijing, are approached over an avenue, the Sacred Way, guarded by a phalanx of stone camels, elephants, lions, horses and assorted strange animals. Actually there are thirteen hidden Tombs of the Ming emperors scattered through the area but the entrances to only two have been discovered — the unfortunate grave diggers were always killed to preserve the secrecy of these underground palaces which contained not only corpses but the immense treasures that the emperors always took with them.

We descended into the spacious Tomb of the Emperor Wan Li who ruled from 1573–1620. It consisted of a series of rooms filled with artifacts. I found the most intriguing feature to be a self-locking device in the vault itself that slipped into place from the inside when the huge marble doors were closed from the outside. A sign put up by the modern Chinese informs us that the cost of this self-aggrandizing tribute would have fed one million peasants rice for six-and-a-half years.

The Chinese government has not opened up the other tomb that has been found, figuring, I suppose, that one of these monstrosities is enough to convince the people of the enormities of feudal exploitation. "We have not time to open up more tombs," Hong observed drily, "although we could do it quickly with dynamite."

Another kind of excavation is not as well known but far more important to the modern Chinese — the defence tunnels in major urban centres.

There were at least 100 clerks in the clothing store on Beijing's Ta-hsilan Street whose 45 stores draw about 80 000 shoppers every day. The manager pushed a button by the counter and a trap door in the floor slid aside. A long set of steps brought us down into a cavern leading into a network of lighted, red brick tunnels that are an integral part of China's defence plans for the urban populations. Piped-in martial music accompanied us as we walked through spacious shelters with eating facilities, kitchens, toilets, generators, ventillating equipment, phones. The Ta-hsilan shelter has 90 entrances and exits and it takes five to six minutes to empty the streets above into the tunnels.

The People's Defence District Manager explained that four million people in Beijing have quick access to a tunnel, all tunnels lead out of the city into the suburbs, and when the civilian populations are evacuated the tunnels will become defence centres for the militia.

"After a bombing attack, we expect to be invaded. We must have manpower to defend China. It was Chairman Mao's brilliant thought to preserve our manpower through the tunnels."

I haven't the slightest idea if the tunnels will be effective or not. They may indeed be a propaganda tool. However, the Australian author Ross Terrill, an expert on China, says he has seen the tunnel system in the port city of Dalian, and reports a construction program under way in Shanghai. What did impress me was the fact that the tunnels were built by hand labour, everyone giving a specified amount of time (after the regular work day) to the backbreaking work of hauling bricks and sand.

To understand where this spirit comes from it is necessary to trace the ideological background of the Chinese Communist Party. The Chinese approach to development was deeply influenced by the course of the Chinese Revolution which brought Mao to power in 1949. Peasants were the base of the revolution, supplying the major part of the human resources for the Party and the army. Two decades of local experience, as the Party gathered momentum before the take-over solidified the conviction that self-reliant development was impossible without a total mobilization of the masses. There had been so much suffering and destitution under the reigns of despots that the masses of people responded to the call of the new Communist leaders to land reform. Millions of peasants felt a quick improvement in their own lives by new policies that broke up huge tracts. Accustomed to being controlled by an authority, good or bad, the Chinese peasants responded to the new idea of organizing themselves collectively. The process of land reform thus led, by continually involving people in the continuing development of the Revolution, to the shaping of new social institutions. Continuous education programs have persuaded the peasants to realize the benefits of cooperation.

The effects of Chinese Communist control of China have been the reunification and strengthening of the country following the disruptive periods under the later dynasties and the penetration by the major powers. The country has also been freed from the factionalism of the warlords and the oppression of the people. The ethnic minorities within China have been given greater freedom and autonomy, education and health care have been extended throughout the country and local people have a greater say in their own affairs. At least that is what the Chinese tell us. Is it all true?

Before leaving Beijing, we were taken to a formal interview with Miss Wang Hairong, Vice-Chairman of Foreign Affairs and a niece of Chairman Mao, who received us in a government guest house, the size of which was no doubt intended to make us properly deferential. Wall-to-wall red carpeting, two chandeliers, murals and tapestries with their delicate Chinese scenes surrounded us as Miss Wang and I sat at opposite ends of a long brown chesterfield. The interpreters and shorthand reporters sat directly behind us. Our Chinese companions sat to Miss Wang's left in positions of seniority, the Canadians to my right. Miss Wang wanted all our questions before she spoke.

Our interview took place at an important political moment for China. Following the death of Mao, a process of "clarification" had started, involving the arrest of four "radical" leaders, Madame Jiangqing, the widow of Mao, Vice Chairman Wang Hung-wen, Vice Premier Zhang Chunqiao, and the ideologist-author Yao Wenyuan. We had observed big-character wall posters denouncing this "Gang of Four" for various anti-Party offenses.

A vicious denunciation of the "radicals" by the "moderates" was underway as the government sought to stabilize itself under Premier Hua Guofeng, very clearly a moderate. These terms, of course, deal with the Chinese political spectrum and not ours. All of China's leaders are Communists and qualify as "radicals" in our terms.

In general the "moderates" believe in technological development, economic growth, increased foreign trade, modern technical education and management techniques, incentives for workers, some private ownership of property, more consumer goods, closer relationships with the United States and the development of China's petroleum industry.

The "radicals," advocating a stricter "Maoist" ideology, emphasize politics over technology. Thus they oppose priority on fringe benefits or material incentives for the workers and want the people to work hard unselfishly for the good of the State. They oppose expansion of international trade and other related activities to preserve the purity of China's revolution.

While he was alive Mao — who always considered contention and uproar to be a sign of revolutionary vitality — balanced the two opposing forces. The communications media, centered in Shanghai, were in the hands of Madame Mao and her "radical" colleagues. But the "moderates" maintained control of the government apparatus and the army. In China power comes out of the barrel of a gun.

The late Premier Zhou Enlai (Chou En-lai) had the personal

prestige to cope with the "radicals" and was able to keep China on course towards mechanization of agriculture by 1980 and major industrial status by the year 2000. But when Zhou died early in 1976, the balance of power shifted to the "radicals," particularly because of Jiangqing's influence with Mao. As soon as Mao died, the "moderates" struck, purging the "Gang of Four."

The unanswered question when our party arrived in China was: How big a following did the "radicals" have? There had been minor uprisings in a few provinces, Shanghai (their home base) was closed for a time to foreigners, and the intensity of the wall poster campaign indicated an extensive effort underway to "educate" the public.

I suspected Miss Wong expected me to lead with a political question, but I wanted to underline the fact that my purpose in coming to China was to study development. I therefore asked her how China intended to concern herself with economic and social development in the Third World, given Ambassador Chiao's speech to the UN which had cited Mao's teaching that "China ought to make a greater contribution to humanity." Actually, Chinese assistance to Third World countries is little-known. The single most important Chinese project is the Tanzam Railway — a 3 250 km. line from Dar es Salaam to the Zambian copper belt completed in 1975 — but there have been an assortment of agricultural, light industrial and community development projects in several African countries and in Pakistan. The aid seems designed to promote trade, increase Beijing political and ideological influence, and counter Soviet advances.

"When we speak of giving support to development in the Third World," Miss Wang said, "we equally emphasize the strengthening of self-reliance. No conditions are attached to Chinese aid which is given in accordance with the Eight Principles proclaimed by Zhou Enlai." These principles revolve around the goal of self-reliance and independent economic development. At the UN and at international conferences, China supports the Third World countries "in opposition to the hegemonic powers' attempts to bully them."

The conference went on for two hours and I kept asking myself: Is all this just form? Is she saying anything? For example, when I asked her about Canadian-Chinese relations, she replied, "They are going fairly well and going forward always," adding that she expected further trade and cultural exchanges that would be mutually beneficial. That seemed suitably vague. Obviously, the "sabotage" of the "Gang of Four" was on her mind even while she reassured me the Central Committee would deal with them adequately. She ended by saying that she had given explanations of principles only, and perhaps these weren't very satisfactory or comprehensive. She quoted "the famous Chinese saying 'Seeing is Believing'" and thought we would learn a good deal during our tour.

Our three companions continue to fascinate us: Hong Yung Sheng, our "responsible person," is deputy division chief of the Institute of Foreign Affairs. An experienced career officer in his late 50's, he shrouds all questions about his background in vague answers. He has a married daughter aged 27, of whom he is proud because she chose a poor area of northeastern China to work in. A son lives at home in Beijing with his wife. The youngest daughter, 17, works in a factory that makes bridges. Clyde said in an aside to me, "I like the way he leans back and appears to take quiet snoozes while others are giving the customary political line, and then he wakes up rather sharply and comes in like an icebreaker."

Wang Liu, the first interpreter, is the most cosmopolitan of the three. He has an amazing grasp of English, even though he has never been outside China. His rendering of long sequences of Chinese explanations, often involving numbers and technical terms, into colloquial English seems effortless. His wife is a Czechoslovakian and works for Beijing Radio.

Chu Pote, the second interpreter, lived in Tanzania for five years at the height of the construction of the Tanzam Railway. A simple, jovial man, who has ten-year-old twins and a younger child, he wonders why we ask so many questions about life in China that he doesn't find particularly interesting.

November 17:
Heroism and
the Red Flag Canal

Linxian, in the mountainous area of Central China, has a population of 70 000. It is, in microcosm, a dramatic example of what modern China is all about. The history of Linxian is filled with feudal oppression, famine and desperate water shortages. Today Linxian is a healthy, thriving community with an abundance of crops and hydroelectric power. The transformation was brought about by the spectacular human effort that built the Red Flag Canal — a waterway that winds 1 500 kilometres through the Taihang Mountains, cutting across 1 250 rocky peaks and boring through 134 tunnels and 150 aqueducts.

In the old days, Linxian was known as "the county of the four poors — poor mountains, poor water, poor fields and poor people." Of the 500 villages in the county, 370 had no water sources. Irrigating the fields was out of the question. Even water for cooking, drinking and animal stock purposes had to be transported from distances of three to ten kilometres. A drought occurred nine years of every ten, and sickness and epidemics were rampant. A century ago a stone tablet was erected which recorded the severe drought of 1877: " . . . people kept alive on persimmon leaves and red soil. They sold their daughters for a few coppers. Deep unrest prevailed."

While the villagers existed in such distress, the landlords and rich peasants controlled private wells. People worked for a bucket of water in pay. Usury was the norm; landlords used small buckets to hand out water and large buckets for the repayment in grain.

These conditions of suffering and exploitation continued until Liberation, which came to Linxian as early as 1944 because of the strong mountain base of Mao's armies.

With the landlords overthrown and land reform instituted, new efforts were made to dig wells and cut channels to bring in water from mountain springs. Mutual aid teams were formed and in 1958 a great collective effort was launched to dig a 10 kilometre trench known as the Hero Canal. Some 8 000 people from 138 co-ops were mobilized for the six-month task. But drought struck again the next year and the canal dried up.

A more ambitious plan was launched to take water from the Changho River which flows out of Shanxi Province and is the northern boundary of Linxian County in Henan Province. In order to build a gravity system, teams went twenty kilometres into Shanxi Province to divert river water along a canal they would build on a contour around and sometimes through parts of the Taihang Mountains.

The battle with the mountains took ten years. At least 30 000 people laboured with pick and shovel, often supplying their own food and sleeping out in the open. At first it was intended to have 100 000 persons each dig one metre. But the roads became so jammed with people and carts that the number of labourers had to be cut back.

A new road, seventy kilometres long, to the head of the canal was built in seven days and nights. Every means of transport available in the county was used to carry grain, vegetables, tools, dynamite and other materials to the frontline of this battle.

Someone painted a huge slogan on a cliff: "*Transform China in the spirit of the Foolish Old Man who removed the Mountains.*" This was a reference to a fable often recounted by Chairman Mao concerning a Foolish Old Man who decided to dig up the two big mountains obstructing the path beyond his doorway. Unshaken in his conviction that he would succeed, the old man went on digging. In the end, according to the fable, God was so moved that he sent down two angels who carried the mountains away on their backs. Likening imperialism and feudalism, which then weighed on the Chinese people, to these two mountains, Mao told China's people: "We must persevere and work increasingly, and we too will touch God's heart. Our God is none other than the masses of the Chinese people. If they stand up and dig together with us, why can't these two mountains be cleared away?"

The first stage completed, the workers faced their toughest obstacle: a granite cliff through which they would have to dig a tunnel more than 600 metres long. To do it, they had nothing except steel rods, sledgehammers and explosives made from ammonium nitrate fertilizer ground finely. A handpicked team of 300 young men and women spent 15 months tunneling through sheer rock from opposite directions. To speed up the work, 20 men, suspended by ropes, worked on the cliff face, opening side tunnels to dislodge rocks. They were rewarded by having their project named the Youth Tunnel.

By 1965 the 70-kilometre trunk canal was finished, and the following year three main branch canals went into operation, the largest of them carrying water another 41 kilometres south, with a flow of .4 cubic metres a second. When the system was completed in 1969, it could irrigate 40 000 hectares of land, or two-thirds of the whole county.

The effects are just as startling as the scope of the enterprise. The barren mountains of Taihang are now green with orchards and woods. Wheat, cabbages and cotton grow in abundance. Intensive cultivation and scientific farming have resulted in two crops a year and a third (winter wheat) in some areas. Intercropping is common. Linxian used to buy 10 000 tonnes of grain from the state every year. Now, after providing for its own needs, it sells 22 500 tonnes to the state each year. And the county itself has 40 000 tonnes of collective grain reserves.

By using water several times over, small power stations have extended electricity to every village. There are now more than 30 small-scale industries producing coal, iron and steel, chemical fertilizers, cement, machinery and textiles.

Linxian's industrial pride is the East Is Red Machine Factory which produces threshing machines, tractors, harvesters and assorted tools — 140 different kinds of equipment in all, 70% of it locally designed. Two shifts a day turned out 1 000 10 h.p. tractors this year compared to 300 last year. Next year's target is 5 000.

Every family is reputed to have bank deposits; universal education to the middle school level is available; the birth rate has fallen from 3% in 1960 to slightly more than 1% today.

We should not conclude that all of China is like Linxian, which is, after all, a special model. But Linxian clearly shows what marvels of development can be accomplished by a people who couple technology with great faith in themselves and determination to strain and sacrifice. It is no wonder that the Red Flag Canal, as Dazhai, draws thousands of people from all parts of China and 80 foreign countries every year to learn from the spirit which inspired its construction.

The Chinese went through a trial-and-error period after the revolution to find the right relationship between agriculture and industry. Some believed that a massive industrial effort had to be made immediately, similar to the Soviet style of development; others insisted on land reform first. Only after 1958's Great Leap Forward did Mao finally articulate the priority that would thenceforth govern China's development: "Agriculture is the basis, industry the leading factor in the economy." This meant that the rhythm of industrial development had to be adapted to the rhythm of agriculture, and industrial production had to meet the needs of agriculture. Thus the policy of "walking on two legs" came into being, with agriculture and industry developing in concert.

In 1960 the Soviets suddenly withdrew aid to the many large-scale, capital-intensive projects under way and this led to the Chinese Communist Party's determination to achieve self-reliance. The state, rigidly controlling the economy in an aggressive display of socialist theory, lowered the price of fertilizer and farm machinery while developing small industries in local areas to meet these needs.

The efficiency of all the new inputs into agriculture — chemical fertilizers, insecticides and high-yield seeds — depends on water. The key to agricultural modernization in China — the basis of the economy — lay in conquering droughts and floods that for centuries affected China. Mao infused this firm policy into the people with such success that it produced an extraordinary enthusiasm for irrigation systems and erosion projects by no means confined to Dazhai and Linxian.

Incredible amounts of labour have been mobilized to construct dikes, drainage projects, reservoirs, dams, sluices, wells, canals and pump stations. During the Great Leap Forward period about 100 million peasants throughout the country were occupied in building waterworks. By 1972, 1 130 000 projects were underway which resulted in the improvement of 3 million hectares. In the North China Plain there has been an upsurge in the number of drainage canals and pumping equipment for many new wells. In the lowlands, rivers have been dredged, new river mouths dug, levees heightened and strengthened and along the rivers, reservoirs built to take the overflow. In 1959 the community of Hengsheng in Hebei Province had one electrically-powered well; today it has 41.

It has been estimated that between 1949 and 1960 the Chinese people dug the equivalent of 960 Suez Canals. By this immense effort the Chinese have freed themselves from fatalistic dependence on their climate and on nature generally. Grain production has risen nationally from 190 million tonnes in 1967 to 280 million tonnes in 1976. All this is a great lesson for the countries of the Third World continually beset by drought and famine.

Our guide through Linxian was Liu Deming who told us he

fled in 1936 at the age of seven into another province to escape famine, while his sister was sold to rich people. Deserted by his father,
Liu was regularly beaten by a landlord. He was 15 when Liberation
came and he returned to Linxian to attend school for the first time.
He got a job with the Communist Party and has become a leading
local figure in Mao's continuing revolution. Now, at 43, he seemed
apologetic that he and his wife have five children, pointing out that
"this was before family planning came along." Eva told him not to
apologize; we have five children too.

Although an ardent supporter of Mao (the day of Mao's death
was the saddest of his life, he said) Liu explained that it was only in
his more mature years that he applied for admission to the Communist Party. Even at age 18, he understood that one should not
put one's own interests first but should work for the well-being of
the people.

"There was so much suffering in the old society that I just
wanted to dedicate myself to working for the new society. If you
just do what appeals to you then we would be going back to the old
society."

As we drove through the villages, which had all benefitted
from new water supplies, I asked Liu if the next step would be to
put water directly into the homes of the people. No, he said, the
priority must be maintained for increasing the production of iron
and steel, more agricultural equipment, coal mining and fertilizer.
Besides, running piping into the clay dwellings would create structural problems for the houses.

The hygiene problem, where people didn't even have access to
water to wash their faces, has been corrected. There are now hospitals in all the communes, clinics in each brigade and barefoot doctors among all the production teams. Even ponds for the children
to swim in are common. Health standards are now high. What Liu
seemed to be saying was that further refinements for individual
comfort could not be placed ahead of the community need for
more production.

When we reached the Youth Tunnel, Liu introduced us to one
of the cliff-hanging heroes, Jen Yangcheng. His name means "nur-
tured by sheep" and he was given it because he was born in a year
of drought when adults weakened and starved, and his milk-less
mother saved his life only by taking him each night to the landlord's sheepfold and finding a ewe that could give him some milk.
We sat on a patio in the warm sunlight, looking up at the cliffs as
he recounted, for the latest visitors, his spiderman exploits dangling
dangerously as he drilled his way through rock. A nearby reservoir
is now stocked with carp and herring. We watched as hundreds of

workers building a spillway below prepared to set off some dynamite.

After lunch Eva, Clyde and I strolled through Linxian's main town by ourselves, exploring side streets and observing how people live. Though spartan, the living standard seemed fairly even among all. The stores were stocked with dry goods, radios, lamps and food. Young girls pulled dozens of handcarts piled with big green cabbages to market. A band of children followed us, but when I raised my camera they ran off giggling.

The advantage of wandering by yourself in China is that you can go where you want; the disadvantage is being unable to communicate with anyone. On one street an old lady in a black dress came up to Eva, holding out her hand and beckoning us inside her small house. It was a two-room clay dwelling with very little furnishing. The most appealing feature was a fire in a stone stove. The lady gently held Eva's hands over the fire for warmth. Then she held Eva's face in her own hands in an affectionate gesture. It was a touching moment, proving that real communication is more than verbal.

"She gave me all she had — the warmth from her fire," Eva said.

November 19:
Christ and Marx in China

Yesterday on the train trip from Anyang to Zhengzhou, Hong came into our compartment to give us more details of our itinerary and stayed to talk about education in China.*

During the exciting upheavals of the revolution that led to Liberation in 1949, Party leaders had lived among the people. But in the first decade of the new life, elitism and the traditional disdain of manual labour crept back in. Many lost their capacity for self-criticism. And within the new generation a large proportion of students were still coming from the old privileged classes.

Mao saw the need to revitalize revolutionary values for successive generations. The reform of education became the cornerstone of the Cultural Revolution which Mao launched in 1966. The Chairman insisted that education took too long and was divorced from reality; city children had greater opportunities than rural students. Mao therefore instituted a new system that would eliminate differences between town and country, workers and peasants, and mental and manual labour.

Students themselves welcomed the changes that led to less bookish education and more equitable career opportunities. But young people became activists in high-level political manoeuvering they did not understand. Their positive response to the education changes became one of Mao's chief instruments in consolidating

---

Even though the subsequent dismantling of the higher education system was one of the most drastic changes in the post-Mao period, I'm retaining this conversation with Hong because it reveals the very educational weakness so quickly changed because it impeded the development of China's intellectual strength.

the Cultural Revolution against the backroom infighting of the time.

Sitting across from us, Hong provided "the three points of education" that we should understand.

First, young people are not admitted to university because they like learning or want a good job. "What we are striving for is to transform man's ideas from self-seeking to being able to contribute better to the revolution." In other words, higher education is to enable an individual to render better service to the people at the direction of state authorities and only those so motivated are accepted.

Second, only those workers, peasants and soldiers who have a certain amount of practical experience are admitted to university. All graduates of middle school (equivalent to our high school) go to the farms or factories to work for at least two years. Then they must be recommended by their peers and approved by the local authorities before admittance to university.

"You have to be judged by those around you as having a genuine desire to serve the people," Hong said. He told us the story of a Beijing student sent to work in Tibet, who ran away because the life was too difficult. "He was a good student but a coward in the face of hardships and difficulties. This illustrates our maxim: If you do not serve the people, the people will not need you."

Third, theory and practice have been integrated. The new system ended bizarre cases of technical graduates unable to operate machines or agriculture graduates unable to distinguish between wheat and rice strains. Students start working in the areas of their academic discipline long before graduation. This has enabled the shortening of courses. Hong said that medical doctors were now being turned out in three to four years of higher education and engineers in three.

Widespread availability of education at the primary and middle school levels and selective higher education, according to Hong, continued to advance Mao's revolution. The thoughts of Chairman Mao had become the basic literacy textbook used by millions of peasants who learned to read only after Liberation. Neighbourhood study sessions for everyone, usually twice a week, maintained the political development of the people.

"The aim of education under Mao," Hong summed up, "is to develop people in an all-round way, morally, intellectually and physically. It is impossible to serve the people without adherence to this correct line."

After Hong's long explanation we began to comment. Bernie thought the interruption between middle school leaving and university entrance was an improvement over our system. But all of us expressed concern about ideology as the motivating force behind education.

Clyde observed, "You have said the interpretation of Mao's correct line is open to discussion. That reassures us. Where can you take us to see this kind of debate?"

Hong smiled. "If you had been at Dazhai during the debates about the uses of agricultural surpluses, you would have seen the vigour of discussion."

"It's admirable to serve others," Eva said, "but creative artists of the past have not had this for a motivation. They believed in art for the sake of art. You neither believe in art for the sake of art nor in education for the sake of education. I worry about that."

I was reminded of a comment Liu, our host in Linxian, made when I asked him what happens to young people who don't want to do as the state directs. "We re-educate them," he said.

Hong slipped back to his compartment as we crossed the wide Yellow River. We rolled by villages comprised of red clay compounds. Washing hung on lines as women did the sweeping. "Those are the first children I've seen just playing for the fun of it," Eva said. Some men were starting to light the evening fires. Off in the distance we could see a military base for helicopters.

We sat talking for a while longer trying to assess our impressions, recognizing that our thoughts were a jumble because everything was coming at us so fast. Hong said few groups had travelled as much by train as ourselves. I much prefer trains to planes because you can get a better feeling of the country. One impression from all the towns and villages we passed was starting to stand out in my mind: there was a general air of action, everyone with energy, moving, doing something; nobody standing or sitting around; no beggars in any of the stations; the fields dotted with work parties. "So much is so great," Eva said, "but what about freedom?"

The little bit we were beginning to grasp about China increased our desire for more information. How are elections held? What about family life? Is there any crime? How is urban development controlled?

The mystique of China struck me suddenly and forcefully later in Zhengzhou where we stopped for a supper break while changing trains. We were taken to a hotel to rest and I caught a shortwave radio broadcast: China had today set off a major nuclear test explosion, the fourth this year. The Chinese government, said the announcer, was determined to break the nuclear monopoly of the superpowers, adding that China's nuclear strength was strictly for defensive purposes.

Immediately my mind went back to the car trip from Linxian to Anyang during which we passed thousands of handcarts piled with coal and grain, many of them pulled by men, others by donkeys — the same sight we had seen on the roads around Dazhai. Both sides and frequently the middle of the road were jammed with the most basic means of transporting vital cargo. It was an unforgettable scene of ordered chaos and Chu, our interpreter, was very annoyed at our exposure to what he called "this backward area."

"It's not backward, it's developing," Bernie told him. "Many societies are over-developed."

"But we've got a long way to go to catch up," Chu said.

Clyde spoke up. "Are you sure we've gone the right way?"

Now, counterpointed against this array of straining Chinese peasants — a feat of the sophisticated technology that commands the power of the atom.

The question of ostensible selflessness in China has been on my mind the past few days. It was Toynbee who said that greed is the glue that holds together Western society. By that he meant that the economy in the industrialized countries demands artificially stimulated consumption to keep the wheels of production rolling. I suppose this is what has led to the materialism of the West. Affluence has become the new ideology in the post-Christian West. Westerners attracted to the undoubted virtues in Mao's China often regard it as a place where selfishness and consumerism have been stamped out in the interest of the common good. But is this a genuine spiritual elevation brought about by a new belief, or is it merely pragmatism the Chinese people accept because they know that frugal gains shared among all have made them so much better off than before the revolution? And as things keep improving, they'll have more? In other words, what do the Chinese people really believe in?

It's easy to see that Mao (at least before criticism of the deification set in) was the god-figure. But Mao said the Chinese people themselves are God. How do you describe this kind of belief? Is Maoism a religion? What has happened to the conventional expression of religion in China, even if it never was very strong.

This morning, on the last leg of our train trip to Nanjing, I told Hong that I was concerned about the Chinese dismissal of religion when, in fact, the Chinese prided themselves on values that were, to me, religious.

"You have said the purpose of education includes the moral development of the individual," I said.

"But I am using the term 'morality' in the sense of proletarian politics," Hong answered. "When people are armed with Marxist

theory and the Maoist spirit, then they have a morality of whole-
hearted service to the people."

"Obviously these terms mean different things to us," I said.
"Let me tell you how I see the relationship between China and the
religion I know. The Chinese people, since the Liberation, have
been taught to have a sense of responsibility towards the community. It is this sense of responsibility that makes possible gains in
water control, food production and so on, and the result is en-
hancement of human dignity in the whole society. But this en-
hancement of human dignity through social concern is precisely
what is taught by Christianity."

I said I found it strange, and unacceptable in the new global
community that the world is becoming, that Chinese and Christians know so little about each other when similar values are held
by each. Culturally and politically the Chinese are the most numerous group on earth, accounting for more than a fifth of the human
race. From the point of view of religion, the most numerous group
are the Christians, who make up perhaps a quarter of the world.
The overlap has always been negligible. Now the point of contact is
practically zero.

"I know that you consider Christianity as something foreign to
China because it was brought here by foreigners and presented in a
Western dress and even identified with colonial powers. But what
you must realize is that just as China has a new perception of itself
under Mao, so too Christianity has gone through its own transformation. Within Christianity, both Catholic and Protestant, there is
a new perception that the Christ of love, who is the centre and the
end of our faith, belongs to every culture and every people and is
not someone who needs to be 'brought'.

"I am not saying that all Christians are perfect exponents of this
ideal of service, any more than you would claim that re-education
is not necessary in China. What I am saying is that it is appalling
for us to be so ignorant of the new reality within each other."

Hong listened for a long time, through several stages of the interpretation. I talked about the points of contact between Marxism
and Christianity in Europe in this new climate of political detente
and religious ecumenism. The old condemnations and persecutions
were by no means forgotten, but at least new efforts were being
made to rebuild a world order.

Then he answered. "I know very little of Christianity. But one
thing is clear. The coming of Christianity to China coincided with
imperialist exploitation and oppression. I would rather think that it
was not Christians responsible for exploitation but imperialists who
utilized Christians for their own purposes. Perhaps the image of
Christianity was distorted by the imperialists in China.

"I know that Chinese orphans were used as guinea pigs to test new medicines. Is this 'love of neighbour?' It was only after Liberation that we found out about many such crimes.

"You should know that in the Constitution adopted after Liberation there is an article guaranteeing freedom of religious belief in China, and freedom not to believe. If you today find decreasing numbers of believers it is not because of a decree by the government but because of the raising of political consciousness out of our own experience."

Hong returned to his theme that the expression "serving the Chinese people" expressed the political concept of class nature. The landlords, rich peasants and counter-revolutionaries are excluded in China as well as imperialists and revisionists abroad. "Serving the people does not therefore embrace all mankind. We are Marxists here and we are engaging in a class struggle."

I responded that my concept of development is to improve the human condition of everyone whether or not I agree with their political or religious beliefs. "I think that coercion is wrong, and if there were no coercion in China, you would see manifestations of religious diversity, including Christianity, among the Chinese themselves."

Hong said, "In China there are some Buddhist temples and monks from the past still operating. But the people don't like it. They don't believe in it. There is a decreasing number of people with religious beliefs."

"Obviously when religion is deliberately phased out, a new generation will have no knowledge of it," I said.

Then Chu spoke up excitedly, intervening with his own thoughts as I had not seen either interpreter do before.

"In the countryside many old men and women still pray to Buddha. But the children laugh at them. Before the Liberation, there was plenty of prayer but a miserable life for the poor. It was only through Mao and the Party that a better life arrived. So it isn't through limitation by the government that religion is eroding; it is because it is useless."

It saddened me to hear Chu parroting the standard Communist line that I have heard in Russia and every Communist country I have visited. How could I respond to a man so oblivious to the hospitals, orphanages and educational institutions opened in his own country in the name of Christianity, to the sacrifices made by so many Christians to be of help to the Chinese, even to the extent of accepting death as 30 000 Christians did in the xenophobic Boxer Rebellion of 1900?

It is true that the Vatican made a tragic mistake in 1704 in barring the Chinese rites that the modern founder of Christianity in China, the Jesuit Matteo Ricci, introduced, thus alienating China's intellectual class. And despite the development of a Chinese clergy in this century (a Chinese cardinal was named in 1946), Christianity was never able to shed its Western dress. Yet the Chinese Communist attack in the early 1950's on such organizations as the Sodality and the Legion of Mary, followed by the jailing of foreign missionaries and suppression of the Chinese clergy, cannot be explained on any other grounds than determination to stamp out a faith that contradicts the avowed atheism of Marxism.

The negative image of Christianity in China despite the altruism of some missionaries, the Communist expulsion of foreigners as the price to be paid for the "humiliations" imperialists wrought on the Chinese, the persecution of religion and the closing of Churches, and yet the evident Christ-like concern for the poor in a society that has rejected religion — all this is a great complexity that must be probed if one is to get an understanding of development in China. The subject demands more than the derision of a Chu or the dismissal by Christians who view with horror the attempts to establish a synthesis of Christ and Marx. In the end, whether development is measured by water control or education levels, the real problem is motivation to set in motion economic and social systems that will help people to develop their own lives. So a belief in something outside the perimeters of one's own life is essential to the question of development.

I returned to Hong. "The world is becoming unified in ways that are beyond the control of either China or Christianity. We should not remain unaffected by each other. Indeed, each is too huge a segment of the whole human reality to be left in isolation from the other. Whether our ideals come from Christ, Marx or Mao, we see a common ideal of unlimited self-giving for the sake of what the common good can obtain through our sacrifice."

"Well," said Hong, "it may be a good idea to have a world community, but I ask you: how can we achieve this under conditions of a fierce contest between the two superpowers expanding their arms and preparing for war?"

Conversations like this are never concluded, they are interrupted. And after two hours of rather heavy give-and-take, I think Hong and I were both glad to see Nanjing out the train window. Our host was the leading officer of the Nanjing Revolutionary Committee of Jiangsu Province, an agreeable man named Shiao Po-hsen who took us on an afternoon tour, stopping first at the Mausoleum of Sun Yat-sen.

This was a delicious bit of irony, since Sun Yat-sen, acknowledged to be the father of the Chinese Republic, was a Christian right up to his death in 1925. I decided not to re-open the religious argument with Hong but to enjoy the grandeur of the structure. An array of pavilions and 392 steps on a hillside lead up to a towering marble statue of Sun Yat-sen with his three principles, Nationalism, Democracy and Socialism, inscribed on surrounding walls.

Sun Yat-sen inspired the anti-Manchu revolution of 1911, became the first president of the new republic, stepped aside in political turmoil and led a second revolution that became the Guomindang (Kuomintang). Admitted to the Guomindang, the Communist Party soon began to take over. By the time Jiang Jieshi (Chiang Kai-shek) broke with the nationalist communist movement, Sun had died.

I was surprised to see such great numbers of Chinese tourists. The top of the hill provided a magnificent view of Nanjing which appeared to be more a forest than a city. Six thousand years of human habitation and containing nearly three million people, Nanjing has a fresh, sylvan glow caused by the 24 million trees planted in the city after Liberation. During a rest stop in one of the pavilions, we were served a warm glass of plum and cassia flower juice that was a delight after an abysmal lunch of Western food at the hotel.

Nanjing is enclosed by a black brick wall, twelve meters high, built as a defence in the Ming dynasty. The heritage seems too valuable to tear down even though it is a traffic obstruction, impeding the flow of iron, steel, machinery and chemical industries that characterize Nanjing's life today.

We found ourselves in a huge park surrounding Hsuan Lake, which contains five flower-covered islands, open-air theatre, play areas for children and a zoo. The park was too big to walk through it all, but we jumped out of the car every few minutes to absorb as much of its beauty as we could. Every so often a couple holding hands could be observed. "This is the first time we've seen romance," said Eva. The centre piece of all the floral displays was an embankment of plum and white crysanthemums in 700 varieties that spelled out: "*Illuminate forever the brilliant thought of Mao Tse-tung.*"

When I told Shiao that no city in Canada has so splendid a park, Wang said to me "Surely you are exaggerating." The avenues back to the hotel blocked with traffic, we detoured through side streets equally congested with bicycles. The houses looked firm and well lighted. The attendant on the floor in our hotel was studying a foreign-language dictionary as we passed.

Then followed the funniest moment of the trip.

Eva, Bernie and I decided to go shopping by ourselves in late afternoon to buy a present for Clyde's birthday tomorrow. We found a small general store several blocks from the hotel and couldn't resist buying a cuspidor, or spittoon as we called them in my youth, those white porcelain bowls that used to be found in all the best places and used for diverse human wastes. Clyde, no doubt, would be properly appreciative, though we decided it would be just as well to avoid mentioning to our Chinese hosts our choice of gift.

We also picked up a couple of colorful thermos bottles, some scarves, a handbag or two — purchases that totalled less than $15. As we poked around the store I noticed that we were gathering an increasing number of young people and even adults who stared at these foreigners who bought things with such abandon. While I thought we were not spending very much money, obviously by local standards we were rich. The onlookers pressed close, though they were very quiet, and now there were about 50 of them.

In a magnanimous gesture intended to further Chinese-Canadian relations, Eva opened her purse and took out a few Canadian flag pins. Suddenly bedlam broke loose. Everyone wanted one, though I doubt very much that the Canadian flag itself produced such demand. As Bernie and I edged our way to the door, Eva had a marvellous time dispensing pins into the clawing, grasping hands. Bernie had a look in his eye that clearly said, let's get out of here before the cops arrive. But Eva was in her glory.

"I didn't know how to tell them that I wanted to save the pins I had left for kindergartens in Shanghai," Eva said as we stumbled along the dark street in great mirth, "so I just kept shouting 'Shanghai.' I'm glad they're human after all."

After the wooden relationship with the Chinese we had been having in public places, and after assurances that a selfless devotion governed all behaviour in the New China, Eva and I were delighted to see the Chinese people with their guard down. Bernie still had misgivings about the mob scene and cautioned us not to read too much into it.

The Jiangsu Province professional troupe was entertaining tonight and our drive to the theatre took us through Nanjing's main square. Adorned with the equivalent of Christmas tree lights, the square looked positively festive compared to the blackness of the rest of the city. The first neon sign that I saw in China was on top of a building proclaiming, "*Let us unite for a great China.*" The theatre was on the shabby side with footmarks on the backs of seats. Tickets, only 40 cents, are obtained only through factories and are in heavy demand.

A string orchestra and a male chorus offered several selections, but the concert was mainly given over to skits and dances with a heavy political overlay. For example, a dance celebrated the installation of electricity in a village and when the first bulb was lit, Chairman Mao's framed face was directly behind it. A pig girl danced to the glories of fatter pigs. The underskirts of the girl dancers were firmly anchored so that in all the swirling the audience saw no more of the feminine mysteries than the ankle-bone.* I could only conclude from the evening that culture has a message in China and the message is Mao.

---

*Post-Mao modernization has affected culture as well as education. In its issue of March 1979 the Far Eastern Economic Review reported; "Imbued with a prudish conservatism under the stringent Maoist-regime Chinese audiences are now witnessing semi-nudity, seduction scenes, inter-racial liaisons and acts of violence in films and on television screens."

November 20:
"Why Are You Asking
So Many Questions?"

The day was long and tiring, the morning spent at the Yangtze Bridge and a clockwork factory and the afternoon devoted to a chemical fibre plant on the outskirts of Nanjing where we also toured the compound housing the workers. We had asked to return to the plant office to put questions to the manager after seeing the operation. The standard procedure for any place we visited was to listen to an opening briefing and then go on tour. By the time we knew enough about whatever was being shown to ask meaningful questions, it was too late — according to the schedule — and we had to be on our way.

This time we were determined to have a long question period at the end of the inspection. How are labour-management relations handled? Are there rewards for increasing production or finding new methods? Is new information shared with similar industries? How do you spell your name and what is your professional background, we asked Keo Hanju, director of the factory's revolutionary committee. Finally, Hong could stand it no more and grumbled, "Why are you asking so many questions?" And Wang exclaimed, "Don't you know it's rude to ask Chinese their names?"

Whereupon we reasserted our desire to learn everything we could about modern China, our intention of making our findings public, and our journalistic background that made us insist on getting names straight. Clearly Hong would be more comfortable just delivering the programmed China message to us. A few days ago he was jokingly inviting us all back for a repeat tour in 1980, to observe even more progress. Lately he hasn't been mentioning the re-invitation.

The Yangtze River, running 5 440 kilometres from its mouth in the Yellow Sea at Shanghai almost as far inland as Tibet, is China's horizontal axis. Dozens of tributaries are themselves major rivers, but the Yangtze is the chief. A myriad of boats from huge freighters to sampans sail along it, picking up and depositing tea and rice and wheat and cotton, the economic basis of 850 million people. In some places it has a golden tone and appears almost as big as the Yellow Sea itself; in others its waters turn into reddish mud. It is power and beauty and danger rolled into one.

At Nanjing, the Yangtze is about one mile across. For generations north-south trains had to be detached and taken one carriage at a time by ferry for a two-hour trip across the river.

During the period of Soviet aid to China in the 1950's a great double-decker bridge was planned, and contracts let for Soviet steel and other specialized equipment. When the Soviet revisionist period struck and their aid programs cancelled, the bridge had only been started. The Chinese determined to find a way to make hard steel varieties themselves. The process was long and the bridge construction drawn out, but in 1968 it was finished. Now it is the pride of Nanjing and a sightseer's delight as 120 trains a day roar across one level and countless trucks the other. "Consequently," our woman guide informed us as we sat high up in one of the towers before a floor-length model of the bridge, "the Chinese people have turned Soviet perfidy into self-reliance."

Or as our local host Shiao Pohsen put it, "Improved transportation has enabled Nanjing to become a producer city instead of a consumer city." The rows of industries we could see on both sides of the Yangtze as we drove across the bridge reflected a growing industrial strength.

The intricacies of watch-making have never particularly fascinated me. Nonetheless for the next hour or so I found myself immersed in a clockwork factory, studying the 60-stage process by which synthetic jewels are made with a tolerance of 1/70 the width of a human hair. It soon became clear that our hosts wished to teach us more than jewel-making, for the factory is another example of the triumph of Chinese self-reliance. Planned by Soviet experts, the factory was designed to use mostly Soviet equipment. Again, when the Soviet-Chinese break came, the factory workers rallied and began designing their own machines. The Russian plant design would have required an expansion seven times greater than the original to reach present levels of production. But "Chinese thrift" enabled the 1 400 workers to reduce capital expansion while still achieving the high production quotas that send spare parts for watches and clocks all over China.

The quotas are set by central planning authorities, the director, Chang Yufu, a 36-year-old former soldier, told us, "but the quota is never as much as the capacity of production. The workers know they are masters of their own factory. They are not working for the individual but for the socialist cause of the Motherland."

An interesting point emerged. The workers, who live mainly in an adjoining factory-run compound at low rentals, receive one day a week off plus eight standard holidays (Red Letter Days) a year. But unless they come from distant areas and want to return to see their families, they receive no vacations. I made no headway raising the psychological point that everyone needs an annual period away from the job.

Over the noon hour we went for another walk by ourselves, up and down side streets as far from the hotel as we could get. The streets and houses were clean. Cabbages were spread out to dry. Washing hung on lines. Children played happily. One young boy with a big smile came up to me and warmly shook my hand. "He's got all the makings of a great politician," I told Bernie. The sight of women pulling heavy carts still amazed me.

Eva was spending the day at a kindergarten and a meeting with teachers. Clyde, Bernie and I set off for the Nanjing Chemical Fibre Plant, 18 kilometres into the suburbs where 2 800 workers produce artificial silk thread made out of cotton seeds that are themselves a waste produce from textile mills. By now the ritual denunciation of the "Gang of Four" and the phrases attesting to the happy rallying of the workers behind Chairman Hua Guofeng, was somewhere between a joke and a bore. Clearly we were being taken to exhibits carefully prepared to impress the foreigner. This is not to suggest that other factories or farming areas are not as productive, for I think the evidence is that they are, but only to emphasize the priority the Chinese assign to political purity.

The factory has its own compound of apartment blocks, kindergartens, shops and recreation areas. Small children in colorful jackets (in contrast to the drab blue of the adults) sang *I love Tian Anmen Square* for us as we passed through the nursery and kindergarten sections. Children as young as 18 months are taken for day care. There was a good supply of games and bedding and a teacher-child ratio that seemed to average 3–40.

Liang Tenying, an attractive woman with short black hair in her early 30's, received us in her flat, which is composed of two rooms, kitchen and toilet. She and her husband and 13-year-old daughter, and her husband's retired father live there for $1.50 a month. A plastic welder assigned to work in this factory, Madame Liang told us the total family income is $65 a month, of which about $40 is required for the basics. We sat in the front room which has a big double bed with blue posts, a bureau, a table and wicker chairs. A big clock on the bureau, flowers attractively arranged and a picture of Mao completed the furnishings. The second room had two beds and a canopy table. Light bulbs were suspended from the ceiling. The kitchen had a coal stove. Baskets of vegetables were piled on a table.

Madame Liang gives the impression of being very content with her life. She cycles to work, watches TV on a community set and meets her friends in the shops and markets of the compound. The rules are set by the neighborhood committee. "But in our family life we are completely independent." Whenever she wants a change of scenery she pedals into Nanjing on her day off.

Rice and the other staples are cheap, and the cost of clothes does not seem too expensive. A cotton-padded heavy jacket costs slightly more than $5, a woman's blouse $4, a man's white shirt $6. Medical care is free in the factory's 15-bed hospital. Dr. Chen Shi-Nen, the staff doctor, said flu, hepatitis and ulcers are the most common ailments. Only 16 babies were born in the compound last year (10 people died), so it is very clear, Dr. Chen said, that family planning is working here. He provides birth control education and dispenses free contraceptives.

The factory manager, Kuo Hanju, was justly proud of the pollution control devices that eliminated poisonous gases and dangerous acids. Flashing lights on his scale model showed the various routings, but we were more interested in the working conditions. The eight levels of pay run from $20 a month to $54, an income that is more attractive when related to cheap living costs and fringe benefits. A 3-in-1 combination of technicians, workers and cadres (those who hold a position of political or administrative authority or responsibility) plan the production themselves as a sort of management-labour council. Our continued probing of the actual process of industrial relations seemed to me to be producing only vague answers. Maybe we're getting tired.

My mood was not improved by Wang informing me, in response to a question about where I could go to church tomorrow, Sunday, that there are no churches in Nanjing, sorry. Christianity was established in Nanjing in 1599 and the diocese of Nanjing was created in 1690. In 1936 Nanjing was put in the care of Chinese clergy. And in 1950, Nanjing had 17 parishes, 47 priests and 32 500 Catholics. Sorry, there are no churches today.

November 21:
The Attractions of Wuxi

China has got to us. At 6:45 a.m. we were on the train, all four of us intensely studying our notes, books and the documents we're accumulating. There's no time to waste. We have to learn more — and more. Everyone is feeling better today, for which we can thank Eva. When we arrived back at the hotel last night, feeling all the frustrations China presents to the visitor, Eva produced a bottle of wine, and stuck a match into an apple for Clyde's birthday cake. Great hilarity ensued as we photographed Clyde with his shining cuspidor on top of his head.

Now a pleasant girl brings us tea as we sit huddled in our coats. It's after November 15 (the decreed date for heat on trains) but the heat still isn't on. Yet the cold doesn't seem to matter. The frosted fields and marshes slide by as the first edge of the rising sun appears over distant hills. A potted yellow chrysanthemum is on our tea table and the voices over the loudspeaker, we are told, are the sound track from a popular film about the daughter of a fisherman who becomes a revolutionary heroine. Our hosts have provided box lunches bearing the inscription "Nanjing Hotel Chinese & Western Refreshments" and inside we find two hard-boiled eggs, thin meat pies, bread, puff pastries and an apple.

For some reason Hong is taking us to Wuxi. Maybe he thinks we need a rest, for Wuxi's chief attraction is resort facilities. The small city straddles the Grand Canal on the northern bank of Lake Tai, one of China's largest lakes. It is also a silk-producing centre.

We suggested that the scenic splendors of Wuxi left no doubt about its tourist potential, but couldn't we get on with visiting communes and work brigades? Patience, Hong admonished us, beauty must be absorbed, clinching his argument with an undefinable logic that insisted our Shanghai program has been cut to give us more time in Wuxi. Eva and I were ensconced in a suite with purple velvet drapes and a pink bathtub as well as a huge balcony overlooking the lake. When I saw it I decided that maybe Hong knew what he was doing. Our resort hotel was certainly not the place to go looking for the average Chinese, but can you blame Hong for wanting us to understand that China has first-class recreation centres as well as roads filled with coal carts?

A rock garden adjoined the hotel. And for an hour after lunch we walked along twisting paths leading around grottos and under foot bridges. The lakes, ponds and rivers in the park all seemed at different levels, each shimmering with the reflection of gold, green and red pagodas with graceful roofs curled and pointing upwards. A pond in the centre marked the changing seasons with four different kinds of trees: plum for spring, flox for summer, caccia for autumn and spice for winter.

Eva stumbled on a stone step, scraping her hand. Hong, Wang and Chu all ran to her. "It's my fault, it's my fault," Wang exclaimed. Eva just laughed it off and put a kleenex over the cut. A short time later, during our briefing at a silk-weaving mill, a doctor suddenly appeared and much to Eva's embarrassment dressed the wound.

Wuxi is another of China's ancient cities (3 200 years old) that apparently only reached its full flowering after the Liberation. Its broad People's Avenue, the main artery for streams of buses and trucks, was little more than a path the width of two rickshaws before the revolution. Now housing has expanded three times. Many new apartment blocks offer an average two-room unit per family renting for about $3 a month.

On our way into the city we passed a long line of students, boys and girls, marching spiritedly to the fields. In this part of China there are three crops a year on 90% of the arable land, providing a food surplus from the regular harvests of rice and wheat. Industry is not allowed on good farm land. Water supply centres are widespread and the rivers improved for navigation.

The shops and markets were crowded and scores of people could be seen reading newspapers posted on walls. We were so used to thousands of cabbages drying in the sun that we hardly noticed them any more.

Before Liberation, our local host, Feng Weichun, told us, there were no schools for the poor. Now Wuxi has a college as well as 240 middle and lower schools with a total enrollment four times greater than before the revolution. There are eight hospitals and sanitaria and the medical personnel has increased four times. In the communes surrounding Wuxi, 200 barefoot doctors have raised the health and hygiene conditions of the whole countryside.

All this development, he said, had been accomplished by following Mao's dictum to make agriculture the foundation and industry the leading factor. In the first stage, 1949–1956, private industries were transformed into state-run enterprises. "In this way industry came into the hands of the real masters, the workers." In the Great Leap Forward, socialist work practices were extended through the development of communes with collective ownership. Production patterns were increased through the state assigning people to fields, factories and universities. Now Wuxi's gross production was 20 times greater than before Liberation. All this in a resort centre?

Of Wuxi's 476 factories, the one chosen for our visit employs 1 500 workers, 80% of them women, making silk thread. Although the factory is 50 years old, it is only with the coming of the communes that the quality of the feeder supply of silk worms has been raised through new scientific methods. At long rows of tables clanking machines operated a railway of carriages allowing each worker to look after 60 cones of twisting thread, each with enough for two suits. In the old days, a worker could only manage 20 cones at a time.

Safety features, free medical benefits, paid maternity leave, pensions (70% of salary for men at age 60 and women at 50) and a six-day week (the factory is closed Tuesdays) had all raised not only morale but the sense of individual achievement, we were assured.

When we stopped at the clinic, Dr. Chu Lenghsun was in the middle of extracting a tooth. Three medical trainees, selected from among the women in the factory, were watching him. One of them hopes to be a gynecologist. Assigned to the factory twenty years ago, Dr. Chu earns $35 a month, about $10 more than the average wage. Most of his work is treating women's diseases as well as intensive birth control courses. When he came to the factory, the birth rate was 3% now it is .6%. Birth control pills, five kinds, are free. Abortions are rare, he said, and considered a very secondary means of birth control. When I asked him about vasectomies he said that, contrary to other developing countries, they were not common anywhere in China that he had heard of.

The two nurseries were not shown to us despite hints that we were interested. I thought this was strange, considering Eva's presence today. I concluded again that they only want to show us what they feel is ready to be seen.

Our hosts wanted to move us along but we wanted information on how workers are selected for education, since we had been told that 26 had just been chosen for a two-year course that would be half work and half study. As the cars waited in the gathering darkness we stood in the courtyard firing questions at the manager, Chang KeChun. The workers themselves had chosen this group, he said, because they had been particularly industrious in exemplifying Mao's teaching. He added that special classes on Marx, Engels and Mao are held at the factory for anyone, and that self-study is encouraged.* Altogether there are some 300 educated youths at work in the factory, i.e., youths who have received some university education and are now assigned here.

"What do you think of the working conditions we have been seeing?" I asked Bernie later.

"What we have seen has been good, but it would be miraculous if every industry in the country were as good."

Eva said, "The working conditions for the women were a little better than I expected. Most of them looked happy."

"Why wouldn't they show us the nurseries?" I asked.

"They probably would not be very pretty by our standards," she said. "The purpose of them is pretty plain, to free women to take part in production. In the process they provide good meals and take care of the health of the children."

"My impression of the living quarters that we have seen so far is that they are not bad," I said.

"In general terms the people seem well-fed and well-clothed, even when we have been walking on the back streets," Eva went on. "Our hosts have admitted that while everyone has shelter there is not enough space."

"Yes," said Bernie, "but don't forget they're only showing us the China they want us to see."

"And screening out what they would rather we didn't see," Clyde added. "While they talk about self-reliance, they seem ashamed of hand carts and canal boats and old houses that Heritage Canada would drool over. Having lived on a boat on the River Thames for two years and being brought up in a 400-year-old cottage in England, I think Wuxi is gorgeous."

"Wuxi," Bernie said, "is obviously a place where most visitors to China like to relax."

"Most normal visitors," I said.

---

*Another result of modernization; factory education programs now emphasize science and technology, not ideology.

November 22:
"The White-Haired Girl"

"I think I know the answer to this question, but let me ask it anyway," I said to the guide showing us through the scenic delights of Lake Tai. The lake is 96 kilometres long and 72 kilometres across with 48 mountains, hosts of cherry blossoms, tea trees and wild flowers providing all the natural beauty that anyone, even our friend Hong, could absorb. The soothing qualities of Lake Tai were undisputed even on this cold day which nonetheless found several couples (the man was often a soldier) holding hands and photographing one another as lovers do around the world. We stopped in one of the lovely pagodas for yet another briefing with more maps and models. I felt the need to ask something different.

"Look," I said, "nearby is the teeming city of Shanghai. Suppose somebody in Shanghai wanted to work extra hard, earn more money and use it to buy a little piece of land on Lake Tai where he would built a cottage for his family. Would you allow that?"

My Canadian companions looked at me with mischievous grins, but our guide seemed nonplussed.

"We don't think anyone in Shanghai would want a private cottage," he said. "All land is owned either by the state or people's communes. There is no permission for an individual to buy or sell land. People from the city come here in groups from their factories a day at a time."

"Well then," I continued, "suppose a man wanted to rent a boat and come out here for a day and fish for fun."

This amused the Canadians even more. The long and short of it, our guide responded, was that while fishing for fun was not exactly banned, there are no boats available and even if our pleasure-seeker found one in the city there would be no way for him to get it to the lake since no one is allowed to have a private vehicle.

My attempts to save what I could of dwindling free enterprise in the world thoroughly quashed, we moved on for tea in the Golden Pine Pagoda. Red mahogany furniture and table tops of pink marble enhanced an already elegant structure. "In the old days," Hong observed, "you could only see furniture like this in the homes of the landlords." Watercolours by Chinese artists adorned the walls. I inquired about the framed lines of cursive script that I had been noticing in various places. Mao's poetry, I learned, has become the object of reverent study. Revolutionary and ideologue, Mao also had a poet's sensitivity. The Foreign Languages Press of Beijing has recently published an English translation of his poems. The one we were looking at in the midst of the joys of Lake Tai read:

Ode to the Plum Blossom
Wind and rain escorted Spring's departure,
Flying snow welcomes Spring's return.
On the ice-clad rock rising high and sheer
A flower blooms sweet and fair.

Sweet and fair, she craves not Spring for herself alone,
To be the harbinger of Spring she is content.
When the mountain flowers are in full bloom
She will smile mingling in their midst.

I found the poetry a refreshing change from the heavy diet of Mao's slogans about grasping the revolution and promoting production that was served up day by day.

Hong wasn't through with us yet. The next item in his tourists' catalogue was a luxury launch complete with tinted glass and button-controlled windows. Twenty upholstered chairs lined the deck. "I don't think I've ever been on a boat as luxurious as this," Clyde was heard to exclaim as we zoomed off to one of the islands noted as the scene of great Spring Festivals. We climbed through groves of peach trees to another teahouse offering a view of Lake Tai in even greater splendor. And on the walls was another verse from Mao:

Nothing is difficult in this world
as long as you dare to scale the heights.

From the viewpoint of a Western visitor, the Grand Canal, with its barges, houseboats and sampans floating by banks teeming with the daily concerns of trading, eating and gossiping, is much more interesting. It was these scenes we wanted to photograph, not the picturesque blandness seen from a launch. The Grand Canal, a 1 600 kilometre waterway connecting Hangzhou with Beijing, was built in sections between the fifth century B.C. and the thirteenth century and continues to be a vital north-south artery.

Our hosts considered this transportation system archaic and not at all fascinating. They were not anxious for us to photograph it but after some importuning on our part, Hong and Feng, our local host, agreed to stop the cars for five minutes on the way to the train.

On a bridge over the canal, a policeman in an elevated pillbox directed bicycles and trucks. Down below on the water crewmen handled the giant tillers on barges, maintaining a steady flow of marine traffic. The crowds of people moving across the bridge presented a vibrant scene and I raised my camera to photograph the strong, determined faces. Hong tapped me on the shoulder. Time to go.

In the car I emphasized again that our point of view was that China was going forward, not backward. Feng still seemed apprehensive about our intentions, although he conceded that our travelling hosts had told him of our serious approach. Most people who come to China are friendly, he added, and the few who aren't can't change anything.

I continued this conversation with Hong on the train and felt him loosen a little. "We still have much to do in transforming the backwardness left over from the old society," he said. "We have enough food and clothing but our mechanization level is still low. We do not have enough living space. We don't have a reception room or a dining room in our houses. A worker's bedroom is still his dining area. And we are still too dependent on donkey carts for transportation."

Our first view of Shanghai was the raucous train station that tells us immediately we have entered an area of China long used to foreigners. The signs are in English, there are special entrances for foreigners, and our local host, a brisk young man named Luo steps forward, greets us in Oxford-flavoured English, motions to the porters and charges off to the idling fleet of cars. No time to waste, he says, you're going to the Shanghai Ballet. A small plaque on the door of the Qing Jiang Hotel informs us that parts of this venerable hospice were created by Gibbons of London & Wolverhampton.

Shanghai evokes visions of intrigue, mystery, romance, all the ingredients Hollywood loves. In truth, Shanghai appears to be a creature of Western commerce, for centuries commanding trade between China and foreigners and within China herself. The lordly seaport, built on the Yangtze basin and the Huang Pu River, must surely be one of the world's greatest. The tall Victorian buildings along the curving Bund — the great commercial street along the waterfront — testify to Shanghai's dominance of the vast hinterland.

As a metropolis of about 11 million persons, including the network of satellite towns and communes that spread out from the core, Shanghai's commercial importance is still evident. Yet in the New China, with development decentralized into strong regional bases, Shanghai is not as decisive as previously.

As the communications centre of China and stronghold of the "Gang of Four," the city seems more diverse and aggressive, much less homogeneous than the other places we have been. Luo seems even more insistent than his predecessors as local hosts in denouncing the infamies of Madame Mao and her colleagues, as if to secure by his insistence the fact that their influence has crumbled. Shanghai is unsettled, the mood of our hosts on the sombre side. We are asked not to photograph the large character posters assailing the Gang of Four lest local people interpret our action as interference in domestic affairs and possibly create an incident with us.

It is not the political mood that we have come to measure, however. We want to know some details of urban planning, for we have heard of the "social transformation" in which Shanghai has overcome housing, pollution and crime problems.

In most of the conglomerate cities of the Third World there is a breakdown in physical and social services caused by overloaded demand when the rural people swarm into the urban centres in search of a better life than they have known on the farms.

But Shanghai has escaped this fate. First of all, the movement of people is strictly controlled by the state. Second, the strong emphasis on rural development has removed the incentive of rural people to seek a better life in the city.

Shanghai is actually sending people out to the countryside as its population figures indicate. In 1965 the birth rate in Shanghai was 2.4% but the natural increase in population was only 1.5%. Ten years later, the birth rate had been cut to .9% and the natural increase was down to .34%. An estimated one million people have emigrated from Shanghai since 1965, part of Mao's plan to "urbanize the countryside and ruralize the cities."

As for social problems, drugs and prostitution are banned (as in all of China) so that today the seaport's reputation as a city of sin belongs to the past when, to quote Luo, "the people were exploited by foreign imperialists and Guomindang reactionaries." Aside from an outright ban on the commercialization of prostitution, the authorities have hit on an ingenious solution to this uni-

56 "THE WHITE-HAIRED GIRL"

versal problem: women do not need the money. Since hardly anyone in China is without a job (everyone not a specialist being assigned to factory or field), women are not forced to degrade themselves to earn money. When the Communists took over in 1949,
prostitutes were rehabilitated.

There is not a single public bar in Shanghai. The movies and
theatre performances are finished at 10:00 p.m. Dull or sublime,
take your choice.

As for pornography, the state does not tolerate the misuse of
its printing and film resources.

Shanghai does not claim to be free of crime, since jails exist,
but the rare sight of policemen and the instinctive safety one feels
on the streets even at night make an impressive impact on a visitor
accustomed to the urban dangers in Western societies.

We suggested that it would be appropriate to meet the urban
planners responsible for this positive kind of development, and received assurances from Luo that he would take this request, which
he found something of a novelty, under advisement.

Shanghai is also the cultural centre of China and the news that
we would be taken to see The White-Haired Girl was greeted by
our group with great enthusiasm. This ballet has long been held up
as the epitome of revolutionized Chinese culture.

Six rows of the theatre were reserved for foreigners and many
British, American, Japanese and Zambian voices could be heard as
we took our places, our interpreters carefully stationing themselves
so that they would have to speak only in one direction. An opening
chorus of men and women in blue jackets and trousers sang three
selections, among them a musical damnation of the "Gang of
Four." The absence of applause for what was clearly a political
message struck me as interesting, considering Luo's protestations.

The choreography of The White-Haired Girl is faultless. The
story opens with the heroine's father killed by a villainous landlord
for refusing to sell his daughter into concubinage as payment for
new usurious levies. The landlord seizes the girl who is beaten as
the man's mother sits praying with her beads before a Buddhist
figure on an altar. The girl escapes to the mountains and hides, living the life of a hermit while her hair turns white. Her boyfriend
back in the home village, meanwhile, has jointed the People's Liberation Army and in the Communist routing of the Guomindang is
part of the army team that liberates the village. Unable to find the
heroine, who is presumed dead, he seeks out the landlord who flees
to the mountains. In the climactic scenes of superlative dancing,
the landlord is captured and the heroine sees her loved one. The
villagers rejoice as the landlord is taken away to be shot. The lov-

ers, with only the slightest touch on the arms to show their affection, depart, he at the head of his regiment, she, rifle in arms, to join the People's Liberation Army.

The applause is ecstatic. The audience is on its feet. The cast returns the acclaim. Wang, who has seen the ballet many times, has tears in his eyes. People run to the stage.

Back in the hotel, the four of us argued about the production and I was the most acrimonious.

"It's too simplistic." I said. "The choreography is marvellous, but the political overload is just too much. I just don't like culture being used for political ends."

The others maintained that it was beautiful ballet, period.

"Besides," I argued, "they are distorting the role of Christianity in China with that scene of the mother praying blithely while the heroine is being beaten. Wang even leaned over to me at that point and said, 'That's how it was, religion was hypocritical.' I'm telling you, it is deliberate deception to identify religion for a new generation as such an evil thing that belongs with the wicked landlords of the pre-Communist past."

"Perhaps," said Clyde, "but the emotion in the audience, people leaning forward on their seats, was terrific. These are the human touches that we will remember and cherish. Bernie and I have decided that we could live in this country if we could see *The White-Haired Girl* once a week."

November 23:
Inside a Commune

There are different ways of describing the 50 000 communes in China that came into operation with the Great Leap Forward. They are agro-industrial complexes. They are a new, more efficient level of administration, midway between a county and a village. They promote local self-sufficiency through collectivization. All of these, a commune is essentially a community organized to pool its resources, production and marketing, educational and health services.

The idea for communes grew out of Mao's determination to repudiate the urban bias of development that has characterized China's development in the early years of Liberation. Not that agriculture had been neglected. Following the revolution, land reform was instituted, but redistribution by itself merely recycled rich and poor peasants, since individuals vary widely in abilities; moreover, often an individual is helpless in dealing with poor soil and insufficient water. Something new was called for to mobilize the strength of the peasantry. Mao called for the transformation of the villages into dynamic socialist centres heralding the new society. The decision to shift the "centre of gravity" back to the countryside was not a rejection of the goal of China to become an industrial power; rather it represented a faith that the human resources for achieving that objective could be found in the countryside. The rural people's communes became the instrument of social change.

The communes were designed to be large, self-sufficient organizations that would arrange all activities — farming, marketing, education, administration, public security — through operating subdivisions of production brigades and production teams. The first three years (1959–61) were particularly difficult and there was a great deal of local unrest and resistance to the changes demanded by the collectivization movement. But gradually the idea took hold as the degree of commune control was reduced and villagers saw their efficiency and standard of life improving through community effort.

Communes developed in different sizes, depending on local geography. Some now number a few hundred families, others 10 000 families. A brigade contains, on the average, about 200 households, a team from twenty to forty households.

The Tao Pu commune we were taken to today is one of the 198 communes in the counties of rural Shanghai, reputed to be the wealthiest communes in China. Described as medium-sized, it has 15 000 people in 3 600 households, divided into eight production brigades and 92 village production teams. The production of food grains and vegetables and seven light industries are its main business.

The manager, Ku Liyung, was ready for us with a barrage of statistics. Yields, piggeries, farm machinery production, bank accounts — everything is up this year, despite a cold summer and delay of the rainy season. The commune not only feeds itself but sells big surpluses to the Shanghai markets, using the cash to buy new equipment that will, in turn, ensure greater yields through multi-cropping. Seven drainage pumping stations have been built.

Unemployment does not exist, since workers are shifted back and forth from farm to factory, depending on the season. Distribution of income follows this formula: from each according to his ability, to each according to his work. Thus each worker is allotted work points according to the authorities' estimation of his attitude to the other members of the team and the quantity and quality of his work. Every child has access to a school. And four barefoot doctors are assigned to each brigade.

Our first stop was a large warehouse, notable for the number of young women doing precision work repairing motors for the commune's tractors. A pump station and canal system were next. Then on to the poultry farm (10 000 eggs per day), the dairy farm and the piggery, all of which looked bountiful to me, although as a city boy I am easily impressed whenever I visit a farm anywhere.

It was the medical centre that aroused my interest for at last I met a barefoot doctor. Like communes, the spread of barefoot doctors has aroused great interest in the West. The development dates from Mao's 1965 directive excoriating his own Ministry of Health for looking after only the privileged in the cities and demanding that medicine shift its focus to the villages. "Our method of training doctors is for the cities," he said, "even though China has more than 500 million peasants. Medical education must be reformed."

Ordering the transfer of medical resources to deal with diseases commonly occurring among the rural 80% of the population, Mao called for the shortening of medical courses and the transfer of half the urban medical personnel to the countryside. This led to a new training program for medical workers, called "barefoot doctors" because they would be drawn from the villages, trained in the treatment and prevention of common rural diseases and remain to practice simple medicine among fellow peasants. This cooperative health care system would be financed through the communes.

The barefoot doctors are not medical assistants but function in their own right after a two-to-three year training program which teaches them to be able to treat about 100 diseases, apply 30 clinical techniques such as blood transfusion and acupuncture and prescribe basic Western and Chinese medicine. A combined work-and-training program enables the barefoot doctors to take responsibility for vaccination programs, health campaigns, birth control education and sanitation work. On top of their health duties, they are expected to work in the fields.

The reported improvements in public health have been astounding. Not only are patients treated quickly in their own surroundings (the more complicated cases turned over to city hospitals) but also the eradication of scourges such as smallpox, plague, cholera and venereal diseases accomplished. The level of hygiene, especially with generally increased water supplies, is now considerably higher than when the populace was subjected to infections by flies, bugs and vermin. Whatever deficiencies exist in the barefoot doctors program seem to be compensated by their greater understanding of the people they live among than the more sophisticated approach of the highly trained doctor who lacks awareness of the patient's social conditions.

Zhao Hsiuchen, a 33-year-old barefoot doctor, greeted us at the Tao Pu medical centre with a warm smile. Anatomy charts, basic medical equipment and jars of herbs surrounded her as she described her life. She was formerly a midwife and perhaps this was the reason, she said, that the authorities felt she would make a barefoot doctor. She spent the first six months in a hospital training program, then alternated between classroom and clinic. There didn't seem much doubt that she enjoys her work, treating colds, bronchitis and the minor ailments of children.

Her husband works in a Shanghai steel mill, returning to the commune only on weekends. When I asked her how many children she has, Chao covered her mouth to stifle a guffaw. "Three," she said, "but that was before we had birth control."

She was so pleasant that I wanted to stay and talk, but our hosts were anxious to move on. A young woman, an accountant, who seemed to be the centre of a seven-person family in a three-room cement-block house, was waiting for us. I felt we were being shown a Chinese model kitchen; for the first time I saw a large, airy kitchen with a porcelain stove with sunken pots and a generous supply of utensils. The windows in all the rooms had glass, another rarity, and the electrical wiring ran along the outside of the walls. A mahogany four-poster bed dominated the main room. Cans of Ma Ling mixed vegetables sat on a counter and a full-length picture of Mao, taken in 1924, adorned a wall. The house is owned by the family and I learned that in many communes it is customary for people to own their own dwellings, even to the extent of receiving financing from a co-op to get started. If communes lead to a new middle class in China, this must be it. The family income is $950 yearly.

The leaders of the local production team (29 households, 114 people) seemed quite comfortable sitting around a table, munching pumpkin seeds and discussing the current agricultural yields. I wondered why some nameless official sat taking notes behind Ku, our local host.

After taking due note of the Tao Pu revolutionary committee's joy at the arrest of the "Gang of Four," we suggested that there must be some problems in even so prosperous a commune. "Yes," Ku conceded, "we are only getting a grain yield of 13.5 tonnes per hectare and we are aiming at 15. And we need more variety in vegetable production." After all, there are only so many times a week you can eat cabbages. Then emerged what I considered a startling statistic. The Tao Pu vegetable fields produce seven crops a year. Plenty of fertilizer, transplanters and manpower prepare the fields for successive growing periods in which vegetables are developed in 25 days. Clyde said later this was possible through bringing vegetables on a long way in nursery plots before transplanting.

Everyone in the commune attends one-hour political education classes twice a week. Is attendance compulsory, I asked? Well, it is one of the factors in determining one's attitude when work points are being assigned.

The urban counterpart of rural communes are the neighbourhood committees and our afternoon was spent in the protectorate of Madame Ma Chufu, an ample and rather severe woman who is the revolutionary director of 45 000 people in 9 900 households in 940 buildings on 317 000 square meters of real estate in the Shanghai neighborhood known as Feng-chen.

As in a commune, a neighborhood committee provides a total

community support system. You are not lost in the big city. You are known, practically everything about you is known, to the neighbours in your block and study group.

The Western concept of privacy seems to be unknown in China, where an individual's personal life, work, problems, health and the state of marital relations are common knowledge. The Neighbourhood Committee is so structured that it provides communal protection; however, signals flow quickly through its network at the first signs of antisocial behaviour. Considering that Western technology has gone to great lengths to give us privacy (a private house, a private car, a private room) that has resulted in a society in which alienation and loneliness are chief characteristics, the Chinese communal neighbourhoods are at least intriguing.

Feng-chen is broken down into nine street committees which oversee the daily operation of the markets, shops, theatres, parks, athletic grounds, kindergartens, schools, medical centre, hospital and light industries that lie in its domain. Madame Ma is proud that Feng-chen has brought 1 500 housewives back into the labour force and that 1 300 aged citizens are scattered through the community.

As an example of the liberated housewife she showed us a light bulb factory that was, in fact, a rather depressing place where the women workers had to do regular eye exercises to relieve the strain of delicate and monotonous assembly-line work.

The out-patient clinic has 30 doctors on staff. The pungent smell of spices in the Chinese herbs led us to the medical dispensary where a boiling process was in operation. When I asked my now familiar question about the local birth rate, I was informed that a decade ago there were 10 000 pupils in nine primary schools in Feng-chen and today there are only 4 000 in seven schools.

An entertainment awaited us in the kindergarten, but I was horrified to see 25 four-year-olds stamping their feet to martial music as, with exaggerated motions, they exterminated the "Gang of Four." Eva says that at a nursery she visited in Nanjing the children, in a similar performance, hurled make-believe grenades at the villainous politicians.

"What we are seeing," she noted, "is children being trained to shoot at whoever is presented as the enemy. The question is: who defines the enemy?"

We considered the scene frightening, yet the Chinese assured us it was in the children's own interest to learn defensive measures. In fairness, the children also danced joyously to the tune *We are going to send tea to the peasants*. The paens of praise to Chairman Mao in the songs and dances further convinced us that the line between education and indoctrination is a thin one in China.

Angry and skeptical, and wanting some Western privacy so I could think for a while, I was ready to quit for the day. But we had one more date. It was with Granny Zhou — who became my unforgettable character.

A kindly lady in her mid-fifties, Granny Zhou lives in a two-room unit on her pension as a retired teacher. She is the cadre, or leader, for 15 families in her block and runs study sessions for the Sunflower Culture group, an after-school organization for 7 to 16-year-olds. For the first time I saw books in a home (all political works) and even a piano.

"Before the Liberation, teachers were looked down on," she told us as she sat on the edge of her bed beside Madame Ma, "but now we are honoured." She was looking forward to the forthcoming wedding of her second son and aspired to visit Beijing to view Chairman Mao's memorial. The fluorescent lights on the ceiling went dark for a few seconds during a power failure, but she went on talking about the political education classes she conducts. Foreigners were not strangers to her.

The standard questions having been asked and the standard answers given, my mind searched for something different to ask.

"What was the last thing you bought that was not a necessity?" I inquired.

"Oh," Granny Zhou whisked some lace off a bit of furniture, "this television set." A portable black-and-white set, costing $122, was unveiled.

"But why do you need a TV set when there are sets in the community rooms?"

"Well, it's nice to lie in bed in your own home and watch TV," she said.

Now there's a universal statement if ever I heard one. Actually, she added, three of the fifteen families in her block have their own sets. Is this the beginning of Chinese consumerism, I wondered.

"Would you like a private car?" I asked.

Our travelling hosts blanched. Hadn't Hsieh at the Foreign Institute told us that, in the interests of conservation, no Chinese citizen would desire a car?

Granny Zhou and her neighbour Granny Zheng, and even Madame Ma, all nodded their heads emphatically.

Although I was delighted to have broken through programmed answers, the reply didn't surprise me. Wherever they live, when people secure enough food, shelter, health and education facilities, they want some of the comforts in life. Obviously making cars, TV sets and other resource-demanding accoutrements available to 850 million Chinese is an unthinkable goal. It is one thing, however, to educate the people to accept the realism of restraint and another to assume that they won't want luxuries after bread. The trick of Maoism, it seems to me, is to make a virtue of necessity. Hailing China's New Man as a selfless servant of the people is too simplistic an appraisal. Yet mixed in with the pragmatism is an undoubted concern by ordinary people for the common good. Even that is a significant step forward in the world society.

We left Granny Zhou's in a great burst of song (the Canadians and Chinese taking turns at the piano), only to have our spirits dampened by the news from Luo that the urban planners were "too busy" to see us, there is no normal school for kindergarten teachers in Shanghai, and the Children's Palace is closed.

November 24:
A City Alive with Human Energy

There can be no more tranquil beginning to a day than to open your hotel window to the sun rising as a great red ball over shining green trees and to look down in the park below where a dozen Chinese are performing *tai chi chuan* the slow, rhythmic ballet movement of arms and legs being exercised for blood circulation. Although it looks easy it is in fact strenuous and the muscles tend to tighten. After a few minutes the participants relax. We have seen this exercise being done individually as well as in groups in many places. It is always beautiful to watch.

Eva and I went for another of our early morning walks. There was motion everywhere, a city alive with human energy. The markets were crowded with fish and meat vendors. Shoppers carried buckets for the fresh vegetables they would buy. Little tea shops served long, twisted doughnuts. On all the side streets, people stepped out of their apartment blocks with pails for the morning water supply at the communal taps. A hundred joggers in formation sailed past us as we studied huge "Gang of Four" posters, remembering not to photograph them. The sight of pale blue brassieres in a store window startled me, so accustomed had I become to shapeless Chinese women in bulky jackets. Fleets of bicycles filled the streets, A hundred or so well-dressed children lined up outside a theatre (at this hour?). Suddenly I spotted a familiar-looking building. We walked into the courtyard and studied the sandstone structure. There was absolutely no doubt that it was once a church. I poked my head inside and saw an army barracks.

Another industrial exhibition was on our agenda, this one at the Palace of Sino-Soviet Friendship. There were major displays of

the Chinese ship-building industry which has, since 1970, increased
production of 15 000-tonne oil drillers used in the Yellow Sea,
dredgers, ice-breakers and ferries. For some reason the classless
Chinese society has five classes on the 858-passenger ferry that
makes the 36-hour trip between Shanghai and Dalian.

Circular knitting machines that produce a nylon glove in eight
minutes, computers, mini-buses, even a huge black limousine with
soft purple seats — the exhibit went on endlessly, and we were still
only on the first floor. "Two-purpose" harvesters for rice and wheat
caught our eye as well as a new rice transplanter which is ten times
faster than transplanting by hand.

Other groups passed us repeatedly as we stopped to ask questions. What's the use of seeing an exhibit if we don't learn something in depth, I told Luo. We would have to skip the rest of the
morning program, he said. I suggested leaving immediately, since
the textiles and consumer goods in the remaining sections were
basically what we had seen at the Guangzhou exhibit. This didn't
please him but I was determined to keep moving.

We went to an out-of-the-way bookstore to buy wall posters
depicting scenes of Chinese life (I bought 25 for $2). The 13-volume
complete works of Stalin, which I didn't buy, sold for $10. When
we returned to our car it was surrounded by dozens of people peer-
ing inside at all the luxury commanded by such important people.

From the roof of the old Shanghai Mansion, 18 floors high, we
viewed the whole city, the few buildings on the Bund towering over
the cluster of red tile roofs jammed together. Although Shanghai
has its own brand of smog in eight layers, the city was noticeably
clearer than New York or Toronto.

Off on a shopping tour of her own, following a day care tour,
Eva returned with a two-string fiddle and we headed for the airport. As we waited in the lounge Clyde set out a newly purchased
Chinese chess set which brought a burst of appreciation from
Hong, Wang and Chu, all, it seems, accomplished players. As a
chess devotee myself, I watched Clyde grappling with the Chinese
rules (everything about the game is different including the four generals who, as defensive players, are not allowed to cross the river in
the middle of the board) but my mind was focussed on how to get
the most out of our last stop in Guangzhou.

Squished into the close configuration of the British-built Tri-
dent Jet, I studied the land below, almost every square metre of it
cultivated, productive as we flew into Guangdong (Kwangtung)
Province, the most densely populated area of the country. Known
in English as Canton, Guangzhou is probably the Chinese city best
known in the West because the twice-yearly Export Commodities

Fair draws traders from around the world. Also the first wave of Chinese immigrants to North America in the late nineteenth century came from this area. Located in the most southern part of the country, Guangzhou is pleasant and warm. Our hotel, the Guangzhou Guest House, a foreign enclave behind high walls with a P.L.A. man at the gate, is set among magnificent palm gardens.

Hong informed us that, as in Shanghai, the urban planners were tied up (it must be their busy season, I said) and the Children's Palace was already booked to receive visitors. Also, no normal school was available. but we would be taken to a middle school and a rural power station. I said we were disappointed that our specific requests were not being met to help us round off our study. Hong said that with so many guests in the country I should understand scheduling difficulties. I got his point and we all repaired to a welcoming dinner given by the vice-chairman of Guangdong Province, Luo-Tien, a big man, suave and knowledgable, who gave every appearance of being able to handle any problem presented by the 50 million people in his territory.

November 25:
The Key to Understanding China

During our tour of No. 61 Middle School, Guangzhou Municipality, we were taken to the Earthquake Forecast Centre where we met forty bright teen-agers engaged in amateur seismology. It is a popular activity at the school. Earth tremors in various parts of Asia are charted on modest equipment. The centre has even been able to forecast earthquakes in China, as the students proudly noted.

When the briefing was finished, I asked, "Is there anyone here who would like to become a professional seismologist?" Ordinarily one would expect that in an eager group of this size at least a few hands would be raised.

No one spoke. Finally, a student whom I had noticed as one of the leaders, answered.

"The needs of the Party come first." The others concurred.

This is just too much for me. Either the students are truly indoctrinated with selfless devotion to the state or they are programmed to give only those answers the authorities want to hear. I can understand the students' willingness to put a few years of service in the fields and factories after graduation, but total self-abnegation does not seem normal to me. Actually I think there is too fine an edge on the declared altruism of the Chinese and under the surface there exists a new generation knowing the way to get ahead is to say the right things.

Madam Li, vice-chairman of the revolutionary committee administering the 2 400 students and 200 teachers, was waiting for us on the steps of the two-storey sprawling complex, surrounded by a retinue of assistants, student leaders, and — a new element — a representative of the "workers propaganda team." A home-made poster greeted us: "Welcome Canadians from Homeland of Dr. Bethune." With the ubiquitous portraits of Mao, along with Marx, Lenin, Engels and Stalin staring at us over tea, the briefing began.

The revolutionary line of Chairman Mao is at the heart of the education system, Madam Li said. Marxism, Leninism and the modern thought of Mao comprise the basic course of instruction, which is kept right up to date, since the "Gang of Four" received the usual tongue-lashing. It was made clear the Maoist philosophy is not something tacked on to the six-hour, six-day school week, but infuses all the academic subjects.

Theory and practice are combined. Students learn the intricacies of agriculture, industry and military affairs by working on the farms, in industries and with the PLA. About a thousand students worked on the harvests in nearby fields this fall. The school itself has three small workshop-factories where such crafts as electroplating are mastered. A farm is maintained in a commune where students grow rice, maize and peanuts and raise animal stock. Physical education, fine arts, and science activities round out a full program.

Sufficiently prepared, students are expected on graduation to respond to Mao's call to go to the countryside and mountain areas to carry on the socialist revolution. "We expect our students to serve the people whole-heartedly," Madam Li said.

The "rustication" movement in which 15-20 million youths were sent to the countryside between 1968–76, is at the heart of China's development model. Presented on ideological grounds of carrying the revolutionary spirit to the peasants, the program is also a chief factor in solving the economic problem of unemployment and the social problem of urban congestion. Last night Guangdong vice-chairman Luo told us that last year 100 000 educated youths were sent out from Guangzhou alone.

The orderly process of deurbanization is not confined to students, as we observed in Shanghai. Ten textile mills have recently been moved from Guangzhou to the rural areas, employees enticed by new housing. Only a good reason, such as family problems, would enable a worker to resist such a transfer.

When Mao insisted that the real power of the transformation of society lay within the peasantry, then it followed that not only should the exodus from the countryside be forcibly stopped but the countryside should be forcibly strengthened, especially by the young in the vigour of their lives. As Mao put it, "By 'urbanization of the countryside and ruralization of the cities' we seek to express the fact that society as a whole is undergoing a new transformation."

Without the "rustication" program, cities would become over-populated with jobless, restive youths bound to create law-and-order problems. By shifting youths outward — challenged to serve the people where the need is greatest — the regime has also economized on the enormous effort in transporting food and goods to the cities. The local production teams have been strengthened with new talent capable of moving into leadership positions. The new talent knows that university will be open only to those who have demonstrated well this desire to serve.

Of course new problems have been created. The new modernization will undoubtedly diminish rustication. Not every urban intellectual makes a good or willing farmer. Conflicts sometimes develop between resettled youths and local workers because of different educational levels and attitudes. There have been reports of youths abandoning the communes and the number of Chinese refugees sneaking into Hong Kong has been swollen by those rebelling against enforced migration.

The total education program, however, is supposed to produce youths who put service before self.

As we toured the school I noticed several maps of the world, China at the centre. In the English class, conducted by a 21-year-old woman, students were called on to read aloud from a grammar containing such phrases as: "We love our great socialist country; we love our great leader Chairman Mao."

Art displays featured former graduates going off to the countryside, their parents giving them a royal send-off into a bright future. In the yard, several classes joined for a calisthenics class, a physical education teacher led the exercises as martial music blared. At the front special steps had been constructed for the convenience of visitors trying to get panoramic shots of this great action scene. The inevitable entertainment awaited us. A 25-piece string and brass orchestra played "The Red Sun is Shining Over Our Frontier," and gay dances celebrated the accomplishments of the Red Guards. In our honour the group sang "Red River Valley" (chosen presumably for its acceptable political colouring) in English, a presentation that called for an appreciation from this politician of growing Chinese-Canadian relations.

Wood and Sanger would rather have spent their time talking to the students to see if at least a glimmer of spontaneity would break through the rote answers. But on the few occasions when an informal conversation could be started, the students seemed either bewildered or bemused by questions on their life that they just took for granted.

Most of the teachers live in an adjoining compound with the

usual low rents. Their salary, about $30 a month, is the industrial average in this area. When we asked again to visit a normal school, Madam Li said they have not been open to visitors since the Cultural Revolution.

Another mammoth water conservation project awaited us at the Hot Springs People's Commune in Tsung Hua County, a ninety-minute drive from Guangzhou. The creation of hydro-electric power has been the main accomplishment here, but the people have had a little fun too. A reservoir and dam were built on the side of the mountain in such a way that if the speed of the water let into the system is increased it overflows into a 75 metre waterfall, a spectacular sight from the road across the valley. We stopped to photograph it on the way up. Coming back, to the great amusement of our hosts, the waterfall had disappeared. Apparently this little game is played regularly by the powerhouse staff who turn the water on and off to delight tourists. My companions insisted that I turn the wheel to start the flow myself so that I would, at last, exercise some real power.

Water, as we have observed everywhere, is a serious business in China. The building of this network of irrigation canals and power stations called for every able-bodied person in the county (pop. 330 000) to give ten days' work to digging the trenches and blasting rock. During the height of the construction, 50 000 people per day laboured with pick and shovel. I asked our guide to repeat the figure to be sure I had it correctly.

When the Russians withdrew their aid, steel was no longer available for turbines. The commune experimented with substitutes and, even though it took eight years, designed a mixture of concrete that made the turbines operable. Now 147 hydroelectric substations in a grid send power flowing through the twelve communes in the county.

The county's rich soil is fully irrigated and farm mechanization is 70% completed. Two crops of rice and a winter crop of wheat and rapeseed are harvested along with the same high-yield vegetable crops that we had seen earlier.

The birth rate has been cut from 4% to 2% in the past decade. Grain is being stored against future needs. Young men train in the militia. Throughout the afternoon references were made to the county's preparations to survive a war. Political education, it was admitted, was lagging a little. Otherwise, life in Tsung Hua County is a Chinese testimony to ingenuity and self-reliance. Even the guest house with its marvellous step-down bathtubs filled with natural hot springs water gave a sense of contentment.

Eva decided to skip dinner, causing consternation among our

hosts. First a maid inquired if she was ill. Then a waiter was dispatched to bring whatever she wanted. Finally Wang came to the room to assure himself that she was all right. No one could understand her not eating when she declared herself perfectly well. "I guess not eating when you're not hungry is too individualistic for the Chinese," Eva observed. As we dined alone, Clyde, Bernie and I joked that perhaps the reason the Chinese did not eat regularly with us was to get a respite from the barrage of questioning. I think also that their menu is simpler than the food preferred to foreigners.

We told Hong that we had a lot of unanswered questions so the whole group gathered for what Clyde described as a "Hong Soliloquy."

The key to understanding China is to recognize that the Communist Party, its philosophy and organization, dominates every element of life, economic, social, military, educational, and cultural. The 2 885-deputy National People's Congress meets only every four or five years to ratify the decisions already taken by the Central Committee of the Communist Party. Fully three-quarters of the deputies are workers, peasants and soldiers; 20% are women; the 54 national minorities are represented; proper proportions of aged, middle-aged and young are maintained. There is the semblance of democratic representation, but election to the Congress is really the result of selection by the Party. The Congress is by no means without value, since it provides a vehicle for channelling discussion of government programs throughout China.

Reconciling centralized planning with the multilayers of administration (the country, province, county, commune, municipality, brigade, village) seems a mystery in China. When we asked Hong how mass confusion is avoided, he launched into a discourse on "the three goings-up and the three comings-down." This involves the establishment of workable production quotas that are first devised at the local level, refined at the regional and consolidated at the national. Then when the national targets are approved the amended plan is sent back the same route. "From the masses to the masses," Hong said, adding that this system ensured that the peasantry understood their vital role in not only producing but also determining what their contribution could realistically be.

Eva expressed her concern about children being taught the ways of violence within the overall framework of service to the people.

Hong reminded us that class struggle is never-ending. While imperialism had been driven from China, the two superpowers were a new threat. The Chinese followed Mao's stricture to dig tunnels, store grain and never seek hegemony.

"We will never attack but if we are attacked we will certainly counter-attack. We therefore educate children to have a passionate love for the motherland and a passionate hatred for the enemy. If we develop children morally, physically and intellectually they will not be aggressive toward other peaceful countries or create social problems in our country. We educate them to serve the people and hate the enemy."

I told Hong that I was frankly impressed that in China I found no inflation problem, no unemployment, no drug problem, no prostitution, no pornography. Social problems that afflict Western countries do not exist, at least on any sizable scale, in China.

"These problems are eliminated by the nature of our society," Hong said.

Then he added a postscript that was a sly reminder to me not to get carried away with the effusions of Granny Zhou. "We don't have private cars or cottages in China and we will not have them in the future. All this is determined by the nature of our society."

The Chinese departed and we were left to ponder the depths of a people so long caricatured as inscrutable. Was I any closer to answering my key question of whether the Chinese model of development was exportable without Maoism? Can only Mao's Communism produce sufficient water supplies? Can basic human needs in developing societies be met without resort to socialist revolution?

Eva said that while she continued to be impressed with the Maoist concept of service, she was increasingly concerned with the lack of individuality and the expression of free will.

"I guess I figure that God gave us free will but Mao doesn't."

Clyde said that our visit to the middle school had thoroughly depressed him. "I just felt creepy about the whole place being so stage-managed. The human-ness of the kids was suppressed."

Bernie shared the frustration about our being channelled into routine inspections. "But I think there is a glimmer of healthy apathy among the masses of students. They seem to have a general expectation in life that they will move up and the next step will be taken care of by somebody."

I was struggling not to have my judgment on the reality of life in China affected by our hosts' eagerness to show us only the success stories. I was irritated by the constant public relations caution that we be exposed only to the politically trustworthy, even in what I felt to be the non-political field of early childhood education.

"Nothing is removed from the intricacies of political struggle in China," Eva said. "Everyone, from children to adults, receives the same political line. There is no evidence that children are being taught to think for themselves. When they learn from the age of two-and-a-half to use violence against someone presented to them as an enemy, and if that line goes astray, that is dangerous. Dissent is discouraged at every level of life, and I see young people growing up who will shoot at whoever is defined as the enemy."

"Eva," Bernie interjected, "you must think these kids are robots, and I just don't buy that. I don't think the kids we saw today are programmed right down the line."

Clyde said, "But at what point is this society going to be confident enough of itself to tolerate dissent? Or is thought control going to be even more perfectly organized here than in the Soviet Union?"

Conformity or individuality? The old question — now in an age beset with the terror of power.

I returned to Hong's insistence on the "nature of the society" as the explanation for social order. "We see the dignity of the human being protected here from those merchants of vice who pander to human weakness in most societies of the world. When I think of what excessive liberty has done to our society, I find many things in China worthy of emulation. But how we can apply the benefits of Maoism to other societies without a constant infusion of thought control is beyond me at this point."

November 26:
"No Quarrel, No Acquaintance"

I think I should state this frankly. Today I had the hell beaten out of me at ping pong by a 13-year-old girl who has been playing the game for only two years.

Several times during the trip I told Hong that I could not possibly leave China without a crack at China's most famous sport (at which I usually manage to hold my own against my 19-year-old son). Don't take on the pros, Hong warned. When we spotted some young people playing at the Children's Palace, Hong indicated that this level of competition was appropriate. Zhung Yiping, a slip of a girl, bowed politely, handed me a bat and then served an ace that was gone before I saw it. Clearly the underdog, I drew the cheers from the gathering crowd, but Yiping's wicked drives, forehand and backhand, drove me into ignominy. I had a grand time, nonetheless, and Yiping tried to soften the blow by admitting she has been practicing a lot lately.

Today, our last full day in China, has been frantic. We wanted to do everything possible to get the last ounce out of this great learning experience. I'm so keyed up I practically got into a fight, a verbal one.

We stopped at the Hua Dong People's Commune, on the way back to Guangzhou, for another inspection of the wonders wrought by water control. As the manager spieled out his statistics, my mind wandered. A bowl of peanuts on the table caught my eye and I asked him if the peanuts were locally produced. Yes, indeed, he said, that was his specialty.

"That's wonderful," I said. "You know, the new president of the United States, Mr. Carter, is a peanut farmer, too. Wouldn't it

be wonderful if your peanuts were the instrument to bring together
the new leader of the U.S. and the new chairman of your country,
Hua Guofeng, in the cause of peace. You would become world famous!'

The manager stared at me. I concluded that he thought I was
mad. Or else my facetious comment had been mangled in translation. Then I remembered the Canadian embassy warning to shun
political humour.

Later in the car our local Guangdong host, a surly man I thoroughly disliked because of his incessant and loud belching, turned
to me. Didn't I realize that the commune manager was just an ordinary person and in no position to deal in international affairs?

I couldn't believe that this man also was taking me seriously. I
gave him a light reply. "Well, peanuts are now in the news and anything can happen."

"But that man could never be host for the President of the
United States," he countered.

"Listen," I said, "the world is in such need of peace that I am in
favour of any vehicle, including peanuts, being used to bring world
leaders together."

When he started criticizing the U.S. as an obstacle to peace, I
could feel my exasperation mounting almost to the boiling point.
"Calm down," Eva whispered. I realized it would be dumb to get
into a shouting match on my last day.

"Well, as our friend Mr. Wang knows," I said, "I have come to
China to study economic and social development and not discuss
politics."

Next, it was Wang's turn to get excited. Clyde, seeing pedal
threshers and 10 h.p. "walking" tractors in operation in the fields,
was desperate to get some photographs for his articles. But his
driver would not stop without authorization. I told Wang to give
the instruction. After the second stop Wang protested that it was
too dangerous to stop on roads that had no shoulders. The scenes
of mothers and children gathering grain were irresistible. Clyde
wanted more and he trudged through the fields. Wang was furious.
"We're responsible for your safety."

I decided it was my turn to smooth things over. When we resumed, I told Wang he must excuse these "frantic foreigners" who
cannot tear themselves away from such an interesting country.

His recovery was quick. "We have a saying in China, 'No
quarrel, no acquaintance.'"

"Yes," I agreed, "now we are acquainted."

We talked about the influence global television will be on all
the peoples of the world when it becomes common for everyone to

see regularly how people live in different societies. For example, the forthcoming Inaugural Address of President Carter should give the Chinese an opportunity to learn what the new president wants to do about peace. Wang doubted that the state-run China network would broadcast the speech live; it would have to be screened first to edit out what the people should not hear and see. The determination of such a sophisticated man to protect the Chinese people against foreign influences shocked me.

We had just seen at the commune a local example of China's media censorship. A small radio station broadcasts news and music. I asked the young woman announcer what the lead items had been on the morning news. The editorial in the *People's Daily* denouncing the "Gang of Four" and the yield figures from the best production brigades in the commune, she said. It is the function of the station, she added, "to carry positive education to the people." The definition of "positive education" is what freedom of information battles throughout the world are all about.

The Children's Palace is a sports and cultural centre attracting thousands of youths every day. A wide range of art, music and dance classes is scheduled every afternoon after school and the instruction is free. Each year 500 students are selected for intensified training in areas where they have shown talent. Handicapped children have special programs. It is altogether an enchanting place revealing the deep concern the Chinese have for the full development, as well as happiness, of children. Special concerts, of course, were arranged for our visit. For the first time I had the impression that creativity had a higher priority than political conformity.

Exhausted yet craving more sights and sounds of the country we would soon leave, we set out on a final walk through the city. The markets were crowded with shoppers hurrying to get home before dark. Eva tried to buy a pair of lovely black slippers, only to find that Chinese slippers are not made for Western feet, or vice versa. There was plenty of clothing in the stores.

Along the streets we could see people preparing their evening meal as we peered into the little houses, some no bigger than cubby holes. There was electricity in most of the dwellings but they were dimly lit. People peeled onions and washed dishes under waterspouts on the street. Though several steps up from a slum, the area was congested and grim. We all agreed that the airiness of life on a commune was far preferable.

Our farewell dinner was a happy affair. We took Hong, Wang and Chu to the North Garden Restaurant, a graceful place with an interior waterfall and called for a private room so we could make speeches at one another. No doubt we had been difficult guests because we never stopped our probing and demands to see more. I liked each one of our hosts and was grateful for the dedicated way they looked after us. Would it ever be possible to bridge the wide gulf that separates us, I wondered. I don't know if it was reciprocal but I felt an affection for them and expressed the desire that they could see Canada the way we have seen China. For the first time with the Chinese we talked at length about our own country and presented them each with a book of colour photographs of Canadian life (portraying our best side, of course).

I toasted my young ping pong friend Yiping and Eva expanded the youth theme:

"My toast is that my daughter and Yiping will one day meet over a cup of Chinese tea — and not over the barrel of a gun."

I suggested that a good subject for their first conversation would be the ultimate purpose of mankind.

Our hosts, as guests for the evening, complimented us profusely on the fine food. In a succession of courses we consumed such delicacies as sea cucumbers, pork dumplings, deep-fried prawns, bean curds, glutinous rice cakes and chicken (I tried not to look at the head). When small whole sparrows, apparently the house specialty, were served, I decided there were certain culinary barriers I could not cross. The dinner, with lots of red wine and *Mao tai*, cost $76. Its success was carried over into another Chinese chess battle between Chu and Clyde. "Remember, gentlemen," I said, "Chairman Mao says there must be friendship first, competition second."

"I thought today was a great day," Clyde beamed as the four of us gathered for a last midnight talk. "We were gloomy last night as we sat around Tsung Hua, then we jumped into the hot springs and things seemed to go better after that. I liked the downplaying of political ideology and the enthusiasm at the Children's Palace."

"Yes," Eva said, "but it too was very programmed and wasn't as spontaneous as I had expected. That's the story of China for me — it's not what I expected it to be. I'm having a real struggle to find the right balance in assessing the positive and negative aspects of China."

"One of the surprises for me," I said, "is that the Chinese do not consider this to be a totally Communist society. The private ownership of homes is a common practice in the communes and there is even a little land reserved for private plots. In fact, the constant emulation of Dazhai, which is certainly an advanced form of collectivism, indicates that much of China is not yet at that stage. The country is not as monolithic as it is imagined."

I said I was still disturbed by Wang's remark about China television not carrying President Carter's address, on the grounds that the good of China had to be protected. "This reflects a deep sense of fear of the intrusion into this society of any ideas that are not totally controlled at the source."

"Let's look at this from their point of view," Clyde said, "just the opening of the doors of China to visitors has been a major step. Take Hong. He's the product of an isolated generation. No wonder he's fearful of our disruptive ways of dashing around talking to everyone. Satellite TV is far more disruptive. It will be a long time before they are flexible."

"This ties in with their development strategy," Bernie noted. "If you want to mobilize a society and get it from Point A to Point B in the shortest possible time, you slam the door. There is wide sentiment in many Third World Countries that they should use this method."

"Again we're back to what is transportable from the Chinese model of development into other developing countries," I said. "The single, most powerful impression on me is what China has done with water. Why don't the Third World countries push water development? Diverting water and building canals and dams is not difficult technologically."

"This is the sort of question you ought to carry to Indonesia and Bangladesh," Clyde said. "The experts there say that if capital were put into harnessing the great rivers, the countries could not only feed a doubled population but become cereal grain exporters as well."

"It seems ridiculous," I said, "to infer that intensive water management projects require a thought-controlled society to produce motivation."

Eva spoke up. "I feel compelled to say something positive. One of the most moving moments for me was the scene in *The White-Haired Girl* depicting the bitter past. People now are so much better off that the things that are bothering us like choices and flexibility and freedom are not missed here because the people never had them. My hope for China is that they will grow to where they will be able to afford the luxury of freedom. It's just possible, however, that there is more freedom here than we think there is. Although not on our terms."

November 27:
The Freedom of Choice

On the train back to Shenzhen (Shumchun), the border crossing point, I felt a little lonely. I couldn't live in such a controlled society. But I wasn't looking forward to my re-entry into the glamorous Western world.

When we said our farewells to our Chinese hosts at the Canton rail station, Hong joked that I would need time for "rehabilitation." He's right. I need some time just to think about all the dimensions of the New China.

In the massive problems of poverty in the Third World, the essence of the struggle is to provide food, shelter, health facilities, education and jobs for everyone in a given society. The West is supposed to make a great many changes in trade and monetary systems to make this possible. Yet China, the most populous country in the world, has accomplished this basic development in the most sweeping manifestation of self-reliance in history.

"That's how I'll remember China." Eva was looking at the clusters of work parties in the terraced fields. In front of me, the wife of a Zambian diplomat held her newborn baby who had appealing eyes and a gorgeous smile. I looked alternately at the fields of workers and the infant. The human struggle goes on. I felt the old pressures returning. The Hong Kong schedule. Messages from my office. Getting caught up on world news.

Eva, in her own reverie, returned to the freedom-security equation. "Does the price of getting rid of social evils de-humanize people by taking away freedom of choice?"

Maybe a certain amount of authoritarianism is necessary, but I agreed with her that it is our ability to make choices that reveals our true humanity.

Eva continued, "If you can't choose what to read, where to go, what to do with your life, if you have to be re-educated every time you raise a question, if you have to buy the line just to go to university — then that is dehumanizing."

I countered, "If you can't get enough to eat no matter now hard you work, if your child dies of dysentry before your eyes, if you live in a shack with not the slightest social security — that too is dehumanizing."

No wonder the development question staggers the mind.

In contrast to almost every other developing country, China has eliminated the worst forms of social misery. Health care, education, and a job appear to be available to the whole populace. All this is "bottom up" development and it provides a human basis for the continued development of China. Yet the Chinese model of development, running roughshod over freedom, as we conceive it, religion and cultural expression, has grave weaknesses. Leaving China I am left with the feeling that we should learn from the Chinese model, not try to transplant it.

Despite the heavy overlay of Communist ideology, there are values in China which a Christian ought simply to recognize as religious values. China shows that self-reliant human development *can* take place when there is sufficient motivation to build up the common good, discipline and self-restraint. While denying the spirit, China reveals spiritual values: therein lies the paradox of Mao's China. What we saw was the development of a new human being willing to subordinate himself to the needs of the society.

PART 2

Indonesia and Bangladesh:
Elitism

December 3:
The Mysteries of the Aid Business

Cars, soldiers and stench are my first impressions of Jakarta. China's parade of bicycles has been replaced by hordes of Datsuns and Toyotas, all in ferocious races with the Vespa motorbikes darting through the traffic. The visibility of Indonesian soldiers throughout the city is a constant reminder that in this military-run regime of President Suharto, there can be no direct criticism of the government or its leaders. The smell comes from the dirty brown water in the hundreds of miles of drainage ditches and open sewers that are open toilets, since only 20% of the city's six million inhabitants have any sort of toilet or sewage facility.

I have to keep adjusting to repeated culture shocks in the modern Asian drama. Peter Johnson, then the jaunty Canadian Ambassador to Indonesia, met me at the airport last night and immediately the problems of development assailed my eyes, ears and nose as we drove past the stinking shanties with their hordes of bedraggled children on our way into the classy boulevards with their new glass buildings and heroic monuments.

Eva, Bernie and Clyde returned to Canada the day after we came out of China. I went to Singapore for a few days to attend meetings of the World Conference of Religion for Peace, an organization that brings together the major religions of the world — Christians, Jews, Muslims, Hindus, Buddhists — to raise the level of religious concern in the issues of human rights, disarmament and development. As I listened to my Asian friends talking about development, I realized their perspective is far deeper than economic progress, which is the criterion most Westerners use. I heard phrases such as "communitarian values of justice and sharing" and "harmony in human society" which reflect concepts of human solidarity. "Besides inner tranquility," the conference president, Archbishop Angelo Fernandes of New Delhi, said, "other Asian values of paramount importance to the process of humanization are simplicity and contentment, non-violence and compassion, cooperation, a spirit of adjustment and a deeply-rooted communion with nature. The Buddhist educator would sum this up as discipline, mental culture and wisdom." The process of humanization, however, is impeded for millions upon millions of people living in immense, resource-poor lands and social systems that protect the few who are rich while doing little to ensure a basic level of development for the masses.

Indonesia must be the strangest piece of national geography in the world. An archipelago nearly 6 000 kilometres long (one-eighth the circumference of the earth), it is composed of 13 667 islands straddling the equator just north of Australia. Most of the islands are not even named, let alone inhabited, and most of the population lives on the islands of Java and Sumatra, which are among the most densely packed areas in the world.

It is a land of Pacific beauty, rugged volcanoes sloping down to tropical forests and thick alluvial swamps bordered by shallow seas and coral reefs. Most of the cultivated land is devoted to rice production, although in the drier sections crops such as corn, cassava and sweet potatoes are grown, and there are sugar, rubber, tea and coffee plantations. Although there is a strong Hindu element, about 90% of the population profess Islam. And while there are hundreds of ethnic groups and languages, Bahasa Indonesia is now taught to students as the common language.

Formerly known as the Dutch East Indies, Indonesia declared its independence from the Netherlands in 1945. Through the 1950's, President Sukarno weathered a series of political crises to form what he called a "Guided Democracy" in which he steered a course between the army bosses and local Communist leaders. For all Sukarno's talk of social change, the old structures, manned by a Western-oriented elite of government officials and military officers, remained unchanged. Which meant that little was done to improve the economic and social conditions of the villagers, who comprise 81% of the population.

In 1965 a band of conspirators, known as "30th September Movement," murdered six army generals in an attempted coup. But General Suharto rebuffed the rebels, blaming the Communists for the trouble. The next few months saw a massive slaughter of Communists and the imprisonment of "social activists." The army forced Sukarno to delegate power to Suharto who began, with the arrival of the 1970's, a fresh effort to develop his country.

Oil had been discovered and visions of the fast buck danced in everyone's head. The reality was that the basic pattern of life in the 58 675 villages hardly changed. Only today the Indonesian government, participating in a meeting in Jakarta of the five ASEAN states (an economic association of Malaysia, the Philippines, Singapore, Thailand and Indonesia), released a survey revealing how desperate is the state of rural poverty.

The floors of 73% of the houses are still of earth, the walls consist of easily destructable material, and there is an almost total absence of latrines, safe water supply and drainage. Consequently, malaria and other communicable diseases are rampant along with diseases causes by nutrition and vitamin deficiencies. The mortality rate is alarmingly high and the average life expectancy only 45 years. Most health facilities, including the 8 279 doctors, are in the cities, far from the villages. And paramedical workers are so scarce there is only one for every 65 000 persons. Two-thirds of all the rural children do not go to school or drop out at an early age. This in turn increases the rolls of the unemployed and underemployed, many of whom head for the cities to try their luck, only to find the slum conditions and joblessness worse than what they left. Indonesia has started a transmigration program in which urban dwellers are given incentives to relocate in redeveloped rural areas, but there are more people flocking into Jakarta each year than transmigration is moving out. It hardly seems surprising that, given these deplorable conditions of life, the average Indonesian has been found by the experts to be lethargic, fatalistic, apathetic and past-oriented.

The government has determined that the preponderance of *swadaya* (traditional) villages be transformed into *swasembada* (advanced), even though the policy will take 25 to 30 years to implement. And to give an impetus to an integrated rural development program the government would like more foreign aid "without strings attached." A national planning agency, BAPPENAS, has set sectoral priorities and encouraged the training of village leaders. But despite these efforts, the Minister of Home Affairs, Amirmachmud, told the ASEAN meeting, "the living standard of millions and millions of our people is still dismally low." Community development, he adds, "will strengthen social political stability."

"That's the very point that they're now recognizing as a result of the Vietnam War," Peter Johnson said as we sat in his office in the embassy. The Canadian embassy is set in a small compound and the staff of eleven officers works behind a bolted door in the reception area. Johnson speaks Bahasa; books and newspapers are piled on his desk and his straight-forward manner gives the impression he knows what he's talking about. "Saigon fell because the South Vietnam government didn't pay enough attention to the economic and social development of the rural people. Development is now the key word in Indonesia." But an even higher priority is given to stabilizing the political order to maintain the confidence of foreign investors. No left-wing nationalizing government will get started here.

Johnson sees Canada's political, trade and aid ties with Indonesia all interlocked. Indonesia's commercial importance in the world is coming up. It belongs to OPEC and the copper and bauxite producers' cartels. It is a growing new market for Western goods. Therefore, it's important for Canada to be in a position to talk to Indonesia. Aid, aside from helping the Indonesians, gets our foot in the door for trade. Creates good will, gives us an entree. If a Canadian consulting firm does a good job on a Canadian International Development Agency (CIDA) contract for a port facility, it can expect to get future business directly from the Indonesian government. It doesn't always work (Canada sent 20 Twin Otters as aid but lost out to a Spanish aircraft for a production contract), yet the figures lead to the conclusion that aid is good business. In 1972, our aid to Indonesia was $18 million and our exports to Indonesia $17 million. In 1975–76 when our aid had risen to $37 million our exports jumped to $78 million. On the other hand, Canada imported only $18 million of products from Indonesia.*

"The political and business spin-offs are immoral to a CIDA philosopher," Johnson concedes. But it is clearly his job to put the whole package together to satisfy the demands of Ottawa which are to place the Canadian interest first. "Aid," the ambassador adds, "is an instrument of foreign policy." This may be devious but not necessarily evil. In fact, a strong case can be made that Canadian aid has responded to transportation, communication, power and water needs of Indonesia. Is it wrong to mix self-interest with humanitarian concern? Moreover, if the Canadian economy falls apart because we're not finding overseas markets for Canadian goods, where will the money for the CIDA budget come from? It's not hard to see why Ottawa's Industry, Trade and Commerce officer in Johnson's office outranks the CIDA team.

The motivation argument obscures an even stronger self-interest factor. Under a Treasury Board directive, 80% of bilateral

---

*In 1977–78, the trade balance was still in Canada's favour, $67.1 million in exports to Indonesia vs. $24.6 million in imports from Indonesia. However, aid had decreased to $13.2 million.

(country to country) aid must be spent in Canada. This means that in 1977–78, when our bilateral budget was $553 million, at least $442.4 million was spent inside Canada. In effect, the bridges, aircraft, generators and assorted big capital items that Canada provides as aid are produced in Canada. This is called "tied aid" and again is readily defended on the grounds that Canadian (rather than foreign) business has a right to the benefits generated by aid. CIDA has contracts with 2 700 Canadian businesses, which is the heart of the message CIDA spokesmen regularly convey to the Chamber of Commerce when enlisting further support of foreign aid.

There is nothing inherently wrong with tied aid, provided that it promotes development. However, given the high technological content of much tied aid, there is increasing evidence that it promotes underdevelopment instead. A myth has grown up that tied aid is important to the Canadian economy; yet tied aid represents only .23% of the gross national product. Canada's "Strategy for International Development Cooperation (1975–1980)" calls for the untying of aid, at least to the extent where receiving countries could use Canadian money to buy goods in other developing (not developed) countries. But Canadian business has fought even this concession and almost no progress in untying has been made.

This is a very delicate subject in aid circles. CIDA is forced to spend the bulk of its money on bilateral tied aid, which usually means heavy technology items, even though its own experts know that the health and education needs in community development should have a higher priority. There is little direct return to Canadian business, however, from this kind of "people development." Consequently most community development work abroad is done by non-governmental organizations (NGO's) that received only 4.2% of CIDA's 1977–78 budget of $1.05 billion. Throughout the decade of the 70's bilateral aid amounted to 60.8% of CIDA expenditures; the second largest chunk (32.6%) is known as multilateral aid and is spent thought the network of United Nations agencies and, of course, the Canadian identity is quickly lost. Though the 1977–78 figures reveal a shift in priorities (bilateral spent 52.9% of CIDA funds and multilateral 39.3%), the greater share still goes to bilateral.

In the case of Indonesia in 1975–76 ($37 million on bilateral aid plus $200 million line of credit), the amount spent on NGO work was only $650 000.

One has to be careful measuring aid effectiveness. It must not be assumed that bilateral aid — because its motivation is "tainted" — does not do some good. Or that only NGO's are working in community development in the rural areas. Canada has social planners, sponsored by the University of British Columbia and the Government of Alberta, studying integrated rural development as part of bilateral aid. A volunteer teacher working with CUSO (Canadian University Service Overseas) under the NGO program is not necessarily making a greater contribution to the country than a Canadian engineer under a CIDA bilateral contract.

The whole aid puzzle has blending pieces. But on the whole, Canadian aid has been oriented to the transfer of Canadian goods and services to developing countries rather than to the development of the self-reliance of the people themselves. Self-reliant development would promote the health, education and marketing needs of the villagers who make up the great majority of the population.

The rich-poor gap is growing not only among nations but within the developing countries. The preponderance of development has been structural or showcase; the first beneficiaries are the elite already at the economic top. The "trickle down" theory has long been sanctified (because it eases the consciences of the rich) but the reality of the afflictions still suffered by the majority has shown that "trickle down" does not work.

Blame for the wrong course of development since the developing nations started winning their political independence after World War II cannot be laid only on the doorsteps of the grasping Western countries. The developing countries themselves shied away from rural development because it is dangerous and not politically profitable.

It is dangerous because it upsets rich landowners who don't want to share their land and who usually have a strong clout with politicians. Tampering with vested interests is high risk for any regime. Also if farm-gate food grain prices are increased the city dweller will pay more, which is but one outcome of the rule of thumb that rural development means less resources for the cities. It is much more politically attractive to build airports, which are immediately impressive, than to mobilize the peasants to build irrigation canals.

On top of all this, the very development of people themselves — awakening their intellectual, physical and spiritual capacities — contains plenty of risk for an authoritarian government unwilling to change the balance of power. Growth creates its own system of power and the re-allocation of the benefits of growth through income redistribution and broadening the social base of development is often seen as a threat by those who have benefitted directly from it.

The Suharto regime launched a big program of capital expenditure to bring infrastructures up to date. Roads, railways, power systems were started, but construction was impeded by a lack of capital and expertise. Donor countries moved in (with far more repayable loans than outright grants) and Indonesia's debt burden skyrocketed. The discovery of oil helped but even though Indonesia became the world's eighth largest oil producer, its financial proceeds from the development of this resource were squandered in the collapse of the state-owned oil company, Pertamina, with total debts of $10 billion, which was more than the national budget. Actually, oil added only $20 to the per capita GNP increase. Moreover, economic gains from oil were wiped out by the higher prices Indonesia has paid to import manufactured goods from the industrialized countries that pass on inflation costs.

Pertamina over-extended itself by getting into such glamorous and expensive projects as a floating fertilizer plant, an airline, office buildings; when the notes from international bankers came due there was no cash. The Pertamina investigation put the spotlight not only on mismanagement but corruption of public officials which is universally regarded in Indonesia as a way of life. *Korupsi* is so bad that everyone budgets for it, even donor agencies knowing they will have to bribe a customs official to get their goods cleared.

"The Canadian government is very concerned about our aid being siphoned into the wrong pockets," Johnson says, "but we do our best to eliminate the danger. It's an acceptable risk for us." President Suharto is said to be displeased because the current clamour over corruption has pinpointed his wife as one of the chief culprits, an allegation by *Newsweek* that doubtless resulted in the banning of that issue.

Indonesia's debt service ratio in relation to export earnings is now at an unbearable 20% which means that money must be shifted from development to debt service. Even though the latest development plan has at last highlighted the merits of rural development to bring up the true economic potential of the country, there is less money to put programs into action. Indonesia needs new aid to help meet the debt service payments on the old aid — while the rice tiller in the fields is still waiting for something to happen out of the old aid to improve his miserable hand-to-mouth existence. The joys of the aid business.

The combination of governments in developing countries wanting Western technology and governments in developed countries wanting to provide it has so far smothered the aspirations of villagers whose need for clean water is considerably more intense than for jets or satellites. Though Canada professes to direct its aid to the poorest, the government is planning two more high-technology projects as a contribution to ASEAN nations jointly: a regional satellite communications system which would provide maritime, aeronautical, television and radio communication, and a regional air transportation study. There is considerable evidence that ASEAN has a greater need of joint river basin development, joint food production programs, and joint environmental management.

Just prior to leaving the External Affairs portfolio, Allan Mac-Eachen flew to Jakarta to sign more loan agreements and remind the Indonesians that economic cooperation would evolve into "a mutually beneficial commercial relationship." Paul Gerin-Lajoie, then the president of CIDA, led a mission to Indonesia a few months earlier which reported widespread malnutrition, over-crowding and lack of basic sanitation and concluded, "The overwhelming impression is of a tremendous need being met by valuable yet hopelessly few developmental projects."

In harmony with the latest Indonesian thinking, CIDA regrouped future aid projects under five main headings: regional development, transportation (particularly civil aviation), natural resources, power and education. Most CIDA aid is highly concessional, either outright grant or interest-free loans with 50 years to repay. Agriculture/water resource programs are to receive the most money. But in the current budget, more of the water resource allocation is for feasibility studies of future projects. A transformation of the countryside by the Indonesians themselves seems a long way off.

The $200 million line of credit, financed largely by the Canadian government's Export Development Corporation, will pay for pipeline, cement and aircraft projects at a blended interest rate of 8.25% over a 13-year period. "EDC is not generous," Johnson agrees, "but we've got to compete in here against the Germans and British and Japanese on business terms."

Neither during nor after their visits to Indonesia did Mac-Eachen or Gerin-Lajoie say a public word about the violations of human rights in Indonesia which have resulted in 55 000 political prisoners detained without trial. Amnesty International has protested the Canadian failure to link a human rights campaign with its economic aid.

The first priorities of the Suharto administration being law and order, the government tried to justify the detaining of political prisoners on remote islands for years on end, as being for their own protection. Social activism was considerably dampened among the populace. A brutal concern for security is a chief characteristic of the government. When I was in Singapore I arranged to interview an Indonesian who had spent two-and-a-half years in a detention camp, his "crime" being participation in demonstrations at the time Sukarno was put under house arrest. Detained under the Subversion Act, he was never given a trial. Only mounting international pressure has forced the government to wind down the campaign. He asked me to have Canada raise its voice. When I related this to Johnson, he said Ottawa felt quiet comments were more effective than public criticism.

After a morning spent in the wierd world of high-level aid, I found it refreshing to visit the Muhammadiyah Vocational Training School on the outskirts of Jakarta. Muhammadiyah is a Moslem social welfare organization, with whom the Unitarian Service Committee of Canada has formed a sort of working partnership. The director, Dr. Kusnadi, took me to a project under construction, a housing unit for about 30 orphan teen-agers, with machinery and car-repair shops attached. Much of the work is being done by volunteers who even gather up the earth displaced by the project for re-sale. The unit costs $32 000, of which CIDA has paid $25 000 and USC the remainder. Muhammadiyah's vocational institutes are well known in Indonesia and are partly funded by grateful graduates who usually get good jobs because of their specialized training.

The staff deemed it unthinkable that I should depart without consuming the Indonesian delicacies specially prepared for my visit. It was mid-afternoon and I didn't need a second lunch of hot, spicy food. But how do you say no? I met the wife of an Indonesian Member of Parliament, a pretty woman in her early 30's who is a family planning instructor.

"How many children do you have?" I asked.

"Six," she replied, "but my parents had 16."

Five children per family is the average in Indonesia, she added. Family planning education encourages couples to have children only with three-year intervals, but no compulsion is used. There are no vasectomy campaigns, as in India and Bangladesh, and abortion is banned, except in extreme health cases.

Dr. Kusnadi, who stopped to recite his Moslem prayers at 4:00 p.m., took me to Aria Putra, another orphanage for younger children, that is the special interest of Dr. Lotta Hitschmanova, director of the Unitarian Service Committee. Of the 46 children, 29 have foster parents in Canada who pay $180 per year towards the care of the child. I read some of the letters the Canadian parents have sent ("I am an engineer specializing in mathematics and I work for the government," one father wrote), reflecting the compassion many Canadians feel about the world's poor even if the intricacies of aid effectiveness escape them.

The traffic jams were even thicker as we drove back in the
dusk. The bicycle taxis, called *betjaks*, were out in full force. A
huge billboard, towering over a refuse-piled street, proclaimed that
Brigit Bardot uses Lux. Gangs of teen-age boys sat on their Vespas,
apparently with nothing to do. I did not see that in China.

December 4:
From Growth to Social Justice

Jack Cox stood on the bank, staring at the collapsed piles in the centre of the river. "I told the Indonesian contractor the supports weren't strong enough," he said, "but he wouldn't listen. I could have stopped him from going ahead but maybe it's better to let him learn the hard way."

Cox is a lanky Canadian engineer spending two years in Indonesia on a CIDA contract to supervise the building of 39 bridges on Sulawesi, one of the major islands, consisting of ranges of mountains that are cut by deep rift valleys, many of which contain rivers and lakes. A CIDA loan of $7.2 million and grant of $1.6 million has partially financed this project.

I flew on a Garuda Indonesian Airways DC-9 to Ujung Pandang, Sulawesi's major city, with Adrian Poplawski, one of the three CIDA officers in the Canadian Embassy, and an Indonesian CIDA officer named Hutabarat. Cox picked us up in his jeep and in an afternoon of bouncing down narrow roads winding through villages, where the bamboo and straw houses were built on stilts, I was able to see three of the bridge sites.

At the first, about a hundred labourers were shovelling earth out of a section of the river bed sealed off from the water. Steel beams from Dominion Bridge in Vancouver were stored on the bank, ready to to be installed once the cement supports were constructed.

Four Indonesian contracting firms are handling the entire project, at a total cost of $15 million. Canadian contractors bid on the job for upwards of $25 million, the much higher figure the result of figuring unskilled labour at what would have to be paid in Canada. Indonesian labourers receive $1 a day plus a meal. "When Indonesian labourers sit around waiting for something to happen, the contractors don't get too excited because it isn't costing them much," said Cox.

The bridge will replace a 60-year-old narrow wood bridge a few yards downstream that sinks 15 centimetres every time a heavy truck crosses it. "If that bridge goes down before we get the new one built," Cox said, looking at the long lines of trucks waiting to get across, "half the economy of this area will be affected." The road is the principal route to Ujung Pandang where farmers unload their rice and vegetable crops and pick up fertilizer, livestock and lumber. Opening more roads and crossing more rivers on routes from southern to northern Sulawesi makes a lot of sense to Cox. "This is a good rice area, but if the farmers can't sell rice they won't grow it, and if they don't have access to markets they can't sell it. I've seen this in many parts of the island. Where the roads are good, the agriculture yield is good."

Cox conceded that red tape and local corruption added to the normal frustrations in the engineering field. When material is imported, 45 signatures of Indonesian customs officers are required for clearance. Their salaries are kept low on the assumption they can increase their income through graft. "Everybody talks about this," Cox said, "although the Canadians stay away from it because we have an agent who gets the signatures and does our clearing."

It was at the second bridge site that Cox shook his head at what he called "a disaster." Actually the collapsed piling occurred at an early stage in the construction and there will be no permanent damage to the structure. But Cox is a professional and does not accept inferior work. Yet he allowed it to happen in the long-range interest of better and faster construction of the whole project. It seemed to me that Cox was promoting self-reliance, which is what aid should be about, even if CIDA would by unhappy at the delay. At the third site, where construction was nine months behind schedule, cranes were lifting steel girders into place while down on the river boys ran a ferry service consisting of a wood platform strapped on top of two skiffs. They charged two cents per crossing.

Driving back to the city, we saw dozens of children riding water buffalo through the rice paddies. "They're not playing games," Cox said. "They're herding the buffalo. That's one of the jobs families give the kids." The roads were filled with women carrying babies on their backs and water jugs on their heads. Coconut and banana trees were plentiful. Washing hung on lines outside the raised houses and underneath animals were tethered and Vespas stored. "Reminds me of my Irish ancestors who shared their houses with pigs," Cox laughed.

In many of the village squares, a large green box was raised up on a post. Community television, I learned, is popular with the villagers who gather every night to watch a mixture of entertainment and educational programs, on birth control, for example. "Bonanza" is a favorite show. "Mission Impossible" was cut out by the authorities because in that detective series too many authoritarian governments are overthrown.

Ujung Pandang was crowded and we had to try three hotels before we could find a vacancy. The Losari Beach Inn was built on the edge of the Java Sea, a scenic attraction that doubtless gave the proprietor the courage to charge $25 a night even though he gave me a room beside a noisy bar and containing the largest insects I have ever seen. We took Cox to dinner at a seafood restaurant where a collection of raw fish are brought to the table. After selection, the fish are cooked and served on a bed of steaming rice. In the Parliamentary Restaurant in Ottawa I've sent back fish cooked with the head on but here it seems out of place to be too squeamish. Anyway, the squid and cod were delicious.

Cox, describing his tours around Sulawesi, expressed the opinion that at least a plan of development is beginning to take hold in Indonesia. The English language newspapers that I have seen in Jakarta confirm this impression. Certainly, development is being discussed everywhere. Back at the hotel I sat on the moonlit lawn, watching freighters gently bobbing in the sea swells and thinking about a lengthy conversation I had had this morning before leaving Jakarta with Dr. Soedjatmoko, a special advisor to BAPPENAS, the national planning agency, and then a member of the Board of Governors of Ottawa's International Development Research Centre. IRDC, set up by an Act of Parliament in 1970, conducts scientific research programs in several parts of the world. Non-Canadians comprise almost half the board. Formerly the Indonesian Ambassador to the United States, Soedjatmoko is regarded as one of the leading authorities in the world on development. Tall and rather patrician, he made a strong impression at the Singapore meeting of the World Conference of Religion for Peace when he gave an address, "Peace, Security and Human Dignity in Asia." I talked to him just as he was preparing to leave for yet another international conference.

The Soedjatmoko thesis is this: "We are now at the beginning of the attempt of the Third World to try to bring about a new international economic order, one which is no longer based on the structural dualism which has kept the Third World in dependency for centuries, but one which would open the way for a more equitable and democratic international order. What we are witnessing at present are the Third World's attempts to organize itself for that struggle, through what some people have called the 'unionization' of the Third World. It is a struggle which may lead to a prolonged period of international tensions, and possibly even breakdowns in the international order, and one which is not likely to end before a major redistribution of power across the globe has taken place that is more equitable to the Third World."

The successful pursuit of a development that is compatible with international social justice and human dignity is the minimum precondition for peace. Development, however, is perceived in two ways. It is the managed transformation of a society, its reorganization and restructuring; as such it deals with government policies enforced through mass mobilization and national discipline. But development is also the emancipation of people, their liberation from obsolete traditional and hierarchical social structures; development in this sense is concerned with human growth, self-fulfilment, initiative and the free assumption of new responsibilities. Of course these two aspects of development have different dynamics which are often contradictory.

Developing countries generally fail to make the transition from the first concept to the second, to move from growth to social justice. While he is much too astute to name any countries, particularly his own, Soedjatmoko has put himself on record with this allusion: "Fear of external threat may lead to the suppression of dissent and blind resistance to necessary and inevitable social change, to the restriction of human rights . . . Some developing countries, incapable of preventing the total polarization of their societies, have gone into a pathological tailspin of escalating violence."

Essentially, what Soedjatmoko is asking is whether strongman rule, which characterizes most Asian nations today, stimulates or stifles true human development. Authoritarian governments provide political stability, thus attracting investment; but they also impede social change and at the first signs of protest the prisons are filled. "The continuing tensions between the need of public order, stability and security, on the one hand, and for continuing social change, with all its dislocations, uncertainties and anxieties, reflect the inner contradictions within the development process itself."

We will all have to learn to manage our fears more effectively and constructively, he adds, and learn to accept the deep uncertainties as part of modern international reality. "It is the kind of courage that only faith and the clarity of a global moral vision can give." With enough vision, he is hopeful that a delicate balance can be obtained between the three points of a development triangle: growth, stability and security, and social justice.

I raised with Soedjatmoko the hypocrisy of so much foreign aid that actually benefits the donor country more than the receiver. "In history," he replied, "many good things have happened for the wrong reasons. It would be disastrous for misplaced idealism to reduce the transfer of resources through aid because continued aid is essential to speed up the development process. Those who make the moral case that aid does not reach the poorest of the poor or is subject to corruption and therefore should be cut off risk being morally arrogant." Aid critics would do better to argue that the transfer of resources be improved through applying all the principles of the New Economic Order. As for corruption, "the idealists in the West" should not assume their own governments have clean hands. Also, to make aid conditional on a government's full respect for human rights may actually result in penalizing the very people whose only crime is to be poor in an authoritarian society. "The problem," he said, "is how to strengthen the freedom of those who are weak."

Soedjatmoko looks to revitalized religious concern with the profound social problems in Asia to articulate the moral dilemmas of our time in ways that are relevant to the policy options realistically available to governments. No nation can survive for long unless it is certain of the righteousness of its course and the morality of its essential purposes. In fact, he says, the Asian nations are coming out of their own Middle Ages and entering a Renaissance period. "What will be the equivalent of the monasteries that kept the flame alive?"

December 5:
"Mr. Roche, Come to the Circle"

It is not only humans who have health problems in developing countries. So do animals. The tic-and-tac disease can quickly wipe out a herd of unvaccinated cattle. Flies transmit the bacteria to horses and buffalo. A chief problem veterinarians face is identifying the bacteria that suddenly develop in remote areas and preparing vaccination programs. This work is carried out by a staff of seven veterinarians at Sulawesi's Animal Health Centre. CIDA has put $950 000 into the project.

The centre was started by the Indonesian government with the help of the United Nations Development Program (UNDP), which funds projects throughout the developing world. It is a big agency and regarded as somewhat cumbersome because of red tape. Its program for Indonesia in the six years 1972–78 includes 144 agriculture, education, social development and transportation projects valued at a total of $144 million. Not long ago UNDP ran into funding problems — more money was committed than actually was available — and some projects had to be cut, including the Animal Health Centre.

From the welcome I received, it was clear the centre's directors view CIDA as their saviour. They gave me a long explanation of what they consider their major accomplishment, the identification of strains causing a liver disease in poultry. There is no vaccination possible and the veterinarians are working to stamp out the disease by genetic selection.

By coincidence today's *Indonesian Observer* published a feature story on the Sulawesi Regional Development Study which Adrian had taken me to visit. For the third Five-Year Development

Plan, beginning in 1980, the Indonesian government wants a master plan integrating economic and social development for all four provinces making up the Island of Sulawesi. CIDA granted $2 million to the study, assigning it to the University of British Columbia which assembled a team of ten social planners. They have recently begun a two-year study to chart Sulawesi's needs over the next 20 years, dividing these needs into three areas: physical resources, including agriculture, land use and irrigation; social development, including health delivery systems, education, transmigration programs; infrastructure, including transportation, port facilities, power, industrial development. Part of the team's job is to train seven "counterparts," i.e., Indonesians who will be able to carry on the project when the Canadians depart and implement the recommendations. But as the *Observer* story notes, finding Indonesians with a background in community development planning has been the Canadians' biggest problem.

Tim Black, a tall anthropologist (Ph.D., Cornell) was in charge when I called and he took me to the compound of new houses where the Canadians live. Although Black was dressed in a *dhoti* and sandals, the group live a Canadian style of life. The wives had prepared an elegant buffet lunch featuring black rice and mango cake.

As an indication of how much development work lies ahead in Sulawesi, the group pointed out that not one road connects any of the provinces, there is no coordination of health services, and only 10% of the cultivable land is irrigated.

The Sulawesi study is similar to one just conducted in East Indonesia by a Government of Alberta team under a $3.5 million CIDA grant. A master plan for the development of 4 000 villages, containing six million people, focussed on the key problem in development apparent throughout the Third World.

"The traditional approach to regional development planning ... has been to designate a set of growth centres and then to rely on 'trickle down' effects to generate positive results in the villages. But the growth centres approach was designed in the West by Western theorists under Western conditions. The theory is based on complete monetization and integration of the national economy, good transportation/communications links between growth centres and their hinterlands, and a relative scarcity of labour. None of the above applies in East Indonesia." Nor anywhere else in Indonesia.

The Alberta team found the basic living conditions of East Indonesia's villagers, who comprise 85% of the population, to be very low: two-thirds of the population is illiterate, half the counties do not have a health centre, the average farmer loses 44 working days a year to illness. While the "top down" approach cannot be ignored, a "bottom up" plan of development was advocated: rural development teams would spread through designated areas giving advice concerning food crops, plantation crops, livestock, health, population control, literature and village infrastructure." Unless integrated rural development is emphasized now by the Indonesian government, the Alberta team warned, the whole nation will face intolerable problems before the turn of the century. "For example, extremely heavy food subsidies may be required by the year 2000 if the measures advocated are not undertaken."

Since the Alberta study was financed under bilateral aid, the contract contained a clause specifying that Canada would be given the right of first refusal on projects resulting from the study. At least the East Indonesia and Sulawesi studies attempt to get at the heart of development. The sick, malnourished villager in the province of Nusa Tenggara is more likely to get some direct benefit from the "bottom up" approach rather than planning a new airport at Jakarta, which is another CIDA project.

"The concept of planning in Indonesia is still quite new," Tim Black said. "There has been so much upheaval in the country that the government is only now getting down to long-range planning." When I asked how the local people felt about the political prisoner issue, the Canadians said they were not permitted to become involved in politically sensitive issues.

Next was a power station where a 14½ megawatt gas turbine was being installed by a Westinghouse engineer from Canada. Four turbines made in Canada were made available by CIDA through a $12 420 000 loan. I was assured by the Indonesian project manager that the additional power fed into the Sulawesi grid would enable new industries to get started. But Adrian seemed doubtful about the priority given turbines as an aid project. So was I, even though it is difficult to argue against power. On our way out the Westinghouse man asked me if I could help his firm get a contract at Biringkassi Port. Here new port and harbour facilities are being constructed to permit the distribution of cement from the $71 million expansion of the Tonasa Cement Plant financed through the Export Development Corporation line of credit.

When I flew back to Jakarta, Ray Verge was waiting for me at the airport. Verge is the administrator of the Alberta Government's $3.7 million International Assistance Program, which supports NGO projects. I had invited him to accompany me in Indonesia and Bangladesh to examine how Alberta's money is being used. The first project was 160 kilometres away in the hills of Cikembar, near the Indian Ocean, and even though it was late we set off with our local host, Wimfred ("Ed') Laliseng.

A 47-year-old Indonesian with a doctorate in economics from Holland, Laliseng directs a program that trains young Indonesian men and women to go into remote villages where they live and work among the people, motivating them to develop their own educational, health and marketing services. About 60 "motivators" have been turned out so far by the six-month training program at Cikembar. The $986 000, three-year project is sponsored by the Indonesian Council of Christian Churches and supported by the World Council of Churches. A major component of church money comes from the Alberta Conference, United Church of Canada, which has raised $117 000; to match this local support the government of Alberta has added a grant of $63 543. CIDA has put in $200 000.

As we drove along a narrow highway in the rain, munching rambutans, a local fruit resembling a pear inside a shell, Laliseng pointed to the rows of foreign-owned chemical and pharmaceutical industries.

"The companies bought up huge tracts of farmland and hired mostly women for their assembly lines. The men, who sold the land because they were so poor, were left with no farmland and no work. The money, of course, was quickly spent. Soon we began to notice a high incidence of mental breakdowns among the men because of the very severe change in their lifestyle. Their wives could not quit hard and boring jobs because that became the only source of income. The men had traded one form of slavery for another. And worse, as Moslems in a male-dominated society they felt they had lost their manhood. The suicide rate went up. This is called progress."

At the moment I felt I was being dominated by Laliseng's driver, obviously an aspirant to the Indianapolis Speedway, who insisted on roaring around sharp turns on the wet pavement in a black night. I poked him three times on the shoulder to tell him to slow down. Cikembar looked wonderful to me, so glad was I to arrive. Laliseng was greeted by shouts from his enthusiastic trainees who served us sweet Java coffee in glasses before leading us to a table laden with rice, peanuts, corn patties, chicken and bananas which they had produced themselves.

Afterwards we gathered in a larger hut, a "workshop" built by the young people in one of their experiments in building earthquake-proof housing. I wanted to sit on a mat with the others but Laliseng called for chairs for us. The official welcome consisted of songs interspersed with special stanzas expressing the group's happiness that we had come to visit. To our surprise they sang "We Shall Overcome" in English. Then they told us about their backgrounds and the villages they would be going to in a few days.

Laliseng asked me to speak. Light from two coal oil lamps flickered across the serious young faces. I said that development was not the importation of Western technology, rather liberation of the human spirit. True development demands belief as a basis. Their project, motivating self-reliance in the villages, is far more valuable to the Indonesian people than another airport somewhere. Verge told them about Alberta and the groups of NGO's in that province sincerely interested in their well-being.

A few members formed a circle and, holding hands, started a slow, rhythmic kicking dance, all the while calling their colleagues, one by one, to join the circle. When I heard the call, "Mr. Roche, come to the circle," it was the nicest moment of my trip.

December 7:
Millions for Planes,
Pennies for Human Development

At 5:30 a.m. Laliseng, Verge and I sat outside the training centre with our glasses of steaming coffee. A torrential rain had fallen overnight. The morning air was pure and the fields a shiny green. After the dirt of Jakarta, Cikembar looked heavenly, although the conditions of life were less than celestial. Already men and women were passing on the road, in search of water, firewood and the round of life-preserving chores that fill their days.

Since the motivator program started, Laliseng said there has been a surplus of volunteers, most in their early 20's. Only those who survive living in a strange village for a month, with no resources, are accepted into the training program.

"Since they are to help the villagers become self-reliant, they must be tough themselves and become de-urbanized. When they are assigned to a village after training, they will face tremendous problems. There are very few health or education facilities. The housing and sanitation conditions are awful. There is no cash for investment in social structures. And many will have to go to their village by canoe, since there are no roads.

"Our motivators need patience, a clear idea of what a village needs and some technical skill to bring it about, and respect for the people's own ways of doing things. They can only encourage. They must not subordinate the villagers or make them dependent. If the villages feel they are being indoctrinated they will not participate.

"Usually the motivators work in teams linking a group of villages to a model village. Small projects are started, such as well-digging, installation of water, credit unions. In two centres we are setting up workshops to adapt tools and machines to local needs."

For a life of hardship, the motivators are subsidised with $18 a month. Some of the motivators have married local girls and have been chosen for positions of village leadership.

The program is still young but Laliseng has done enough field supervision to convince himself that the results obtained so far in 47 villages justify its continuance beyond the three-year initial funding period. He has to worry not only about the demands of the training program but about a rearguard within the Christian churches opposed to using "Christian" money to help "Moslem" villagers.

We climbed a hill behind the centre to the dormitories and dining hall. One of the cottages with a roof of palm leaves was named "Albert Schweitzer." The trainees sleep on straw mats, save human and animal wastes to make methane gas, and have set up a windmill to pump water. Laliseng showed us a grove of fruit trees that had been planted and the inter-cropping of peanuts and corn.

"They will never be hungry if they know how to grow their own food."

We went into the hall for a prayer service and a breakfast of fish, rice and tea. Then Laliseng rose for his farewell. Those about to leave for the villages joined hands with Laliseng in a circle. He gripped each one by the arm in an emotional goodbye. I knew I could not join that circle.

On the way back to Jakarta, Laliseng said INCO had offered him a job at ten times his present salary. It was a struggle to turn it down because he has five children in teen-age and college years. "But I didn't want to give up my freedom for slavery."

Within a few hours, Verge and I were catapulted across centuries. From village canoes to screaming jets. We spent the afternoon at the Curug Civil Aviation Training Centre at Budiarto airfield, a twenty-minute flight from Jakarta's municipal airport. Opening up Indonesia by air service has been a priority of the Indonesian government and, for several years, Canada has been a major supporter of the training centre. CIDA provided a $25 million loan for navigational equipment, consulting services from Aviation Planning Services (Montreal) for a masterplan for a new airport at Jakarta, a fleet of Twin Otters and communications equipment. In addition CIDA donated nearly $1 million to upgrade the training centre and provide facilities for English-language training for pilots. This had to be followed by a special grant of $50 000 to improve the water supply system for the additional trainees.

The Indonesian government wants 500 more Indonesian pilots

before 1981; at the moment the country is overly dependent on foreign commercial pilots. The training centre currently has 135 students, who are the lucky few chosen from a rigid screening process. We were given a tour of the school with overhead projection slides and reams of statistics thrown in to indicate the importance of this work in extending commerce and tourism in Indonesia. An immediate goal is a jet freighter service linking Jakarta and North America.

The centre is not without its problems, however. The language training equipment was broken and the contract with the Canadian supplier did not cover repairs (new equipment from Japan is on order). Signs of rust were on a fire fighting truck and the log on a turbine testing machine revealed it had been used only three times in the past four months.

An instructor gave us an aerial tour of Jakarta. Down below the city was a sea of red clay roofs. I thought about where I would put development money — into the Cikembar centre or pilot training? Will opening up the remote areas to air service relieve the population pressure in Jakarta and lead to more even social development? I doubt it. But can Indonesia turn its back on the air age and hope to become an important industrial country? No. Does being an important industrial country spell development? Back to Cikembar. Small is beautiful but big is necessary. The return of the world to a pastoral society is a romantic illusion. Development has many sides. "Top down" and "bottom up!" It's both. We have to try to see development from the Asian point of view. Indonesia needs technology as well as community development.

But if we truly want to help Indonesians to develop rather than helping ourselves with tied aid, we will put much more money into community development. It is a question of changing our own priorities to give more than lip service to the basic life-support needs of the world's villagers. Millions for generators and aircraft; pennies for human needs. That is our present philosophy. U.S. President John F. Kennedy once said that life is unfair. The development process is unfair.

A few minutes after landing I went on a tour of Jakarta and made myself walk through some of the vilest slums I have ever seen in the Third World. Fifty per cent of Jakarta lives at the subsistence level, but the deep dimensions of this poverty cannot be seen from the air. Now I was down in the squalour and smells.

Hundreds of shacks are wedged together on the bank of a canal. The people are squatters, their only possessions a few dirty utensils. Within a block I count 75 children. There is not a bit of play area. They are unkempt. Many have the big belly that comes from malnutrition.

Here is a woman in a polka dot dress sitting on the road eating a plate of rice. I think of her transformed into a blonde beauty dining in a fancy restaurant at home. Why will she never be transformed? Would she possess more human dignity if she were?

There is a man defecating into the canal. Does he not know any better? Where else is there to go? In my home there are two full bathrooms, and I get annoyed if they are not perfectly clean.

A mother and son sit beside an open sewer. A man operates a sewing machine outside his hut. A boy whistles as he delivers his newspapers. A family is cooking fish on an open fire.

Up a set of stone steps is an open-air bazaar, crowded as people strain to see the trinkets hawkers are peddling. It is a blaze of colour and a skilful photographer could make this an enchanting native scene. Actually the stands are full of junk, and the only useful items are the bathtubs and toilets on display.

Across the street is the Vilini Hair Dresser and Beauty Parlour and an open air restaurant. I don't think I'll eat there. The houses are a little better in this section. They are dingy but not dilapidated. A teen-age girl combs her hair in the glass-less window. A yellow taxi with a light on top goes by. A man in a green cap rides by on his Vespa. A girl in a red dress behind holding onto him. "Sampson and Delilah" is playing at the Riang Theatre. The crowds are thick on every street.

I want to see another section of Jakarta. It can't all be slums, although God knows there are enough of them. I go to a suburb called Tebet. The streets are narrow, but there are individual homes, banana trees, flowers, electricity. No one is cooking outside. But there is no city water in this section and people have to cart pails several blocks. There is a beautiful woman of about 20 with a child in her arms. Six betjak drivers are waiting on a corner for fares. The lights are starting to come on. People are sitting outside a health clinic. Maybe it will open.

The six-lane Kuningen Boulevard sweeps me back to my clean sheets, dinnerware, well-cooked food, wine, and most of all to a peaceful setting in a room by myself where I can think about the contradictions of the modern world. I never want to see those slums again, but I keep wondering if that kid I saw scrounging in some garbage is getting a meal tonight.

December 8:
The Spectacular Mistakes
of Indonesia

Today, while I was driving between appointments an embassy officer reached into his briefcase and pulled out a nine-page document typed single-space.

"You can read this once, but you may not take notes from it," he said, speaking softly so the driver would not hear. I had five minutes before we reached the next stop.

The document was a confidential memorandum to External Affairs in Ottawa, detailing the terrible housing, health and education facilities in Indonesia. It said the Indonesian government was still star-struck on prestige projects. Canadian aid should be shifted away from these to reinforce community planning in the villages and transmigration programs. Despite some good programs, the bulk of Canadian aid is clearly benefitting the elite while conditions of life for the poor are worsening. The document recommended a tougher Canadian approach to aid, acknowledging that such a redirection would have little commercial benefit to Canada.

Ottawa didn't want the document made public, the officer said, because it made a mockery of the humanitarian front the government puts up to cover our real interest in foreign aid.

Later, at a staff meeting at the embassy, I pointed out that the aid and trade figures made it evident that Canada is the net beneficee, not benefactor, in our relations with Indonesia. And the same situation obtains in many developing countries.

"That is an irresponsible statement," said the embassy's trade counsellor. "One quarter of Canada's GNP is derived from trade.

We operate as a multinational trading company. After all, we have to make a living. Developing trade just makes good sense." He backed up his argument with some figures that ought to make me, an Alberta politician, very happy. Of six contracts obtained by Canadian companies for construction and drilling work in Indonesia, totalling $178 million and all backed by the Export Development Corporation, three totalling $45 million are with Alberta-based companies. Canadian companies are currently pursuing $300 million in new projects authorized by the Indonesian government. The trade counsellor concluded his argument, "Aid gives market exposure for Canadian products."

The CIDA officers looked uncomfortable. They recognized the reality — in hard political domestic terms — of the counsellor's position. In any event they do not make government policy. Their job is to administer the aid Ottawa approves. They acknowledged that, with only three aid officers to administer a $37 million program, evaluation was virtually impossible. If they can assure Ottawa that no one is stealing the money, that is as much checking as can be expected. To monitor the real effect of aid — whether the lives of people are actually improved and how — would require far more time and tools than they possess. They claimed it is false economy for Canada to maintain such a low ratio of CIDA staff in the field (90% of CIDA's staff is in Ottawa). The Americans maintain a much higher proportion of aid officers in the field.

Ambassador Johnson is against expanding the local staff because it costs the Canadian government at least $200 000 a year just to house each Canadian officer because of Indonesia's inflationary economy. Paul Gerin-Lajoie, CIDA's president, complained in his report about the exorbitant housing costs in Jakarta, where rents range as high as $2 000 a month. "If we are to carry out an effective program emphasizing the transfer of technology, these difficulties in placing Canadian experts in Indonesia must be removed." Johnson's opposition goes beyond costs. Too many government departments, including CIDA, want to get their own people into the field overseas. If tight control is not maintained by the Canadian ambassador over all Canadian activities in a country, chaos results.

Without adequate tools for measuring aid effectiveness, the next best thing is CIDA's "Country Report," a document that relates the existing and planned projects in the context of the need as it has been analyzed. The Standing Committee on External Affairs and National Defence in Parliament has long sought these reports in order that M.P.s could give a balanced judgment on CIDA's performance when estimates for the coming year come up for parliamentary approval. CIDA has always resisted releasing the reports on the grounds that they contain confidential analyses that might prove embarrassing if made public. It has never been clear to me if the embarrassment would be suffered more by the receiving country or by Ottawa. I was not surprised, therefore, when the embassy refused to show me the Country Report on Indonesia.

Aid is such a grab-bag of wheeling-and-dealing, with a dash of humanitarianism thrown in, that no clear result of its effectiveness is possible. In fact at a meeting this morning, Dr. Saleh Afiff, deputy director of BAPPENAS, said that aid is ceasing to be important to Indonesia; 87% of the $3.2 billion community and rural development budget is provided by the Government of Indonesia whereas a few years ago development funds were obtained almost exclusively from foreign aid. Canadian aid is such a small part of the development process that its continuance is not of great significance. Dr. Afiff did not mean to be insulting. His approach was simply business-like, no different from Canada's. Of course, he added, Indonesia preferred to retain Canadian support because if we dropped away, other industrialized countries might follow.

"The real way for Canada to help us," he said, "would be to finance our local costs for rural development. I don't mean that you should participate in this development. We don't need Western technology in rural areas. We know better than you what we need. But the Canadian government does not provide much aid on this no-strings attached basis. Therefore, we accept your aid in the form of big technology items which we need anyway, although it would be cheaper for us to be able to buy these items elsewhere. Because of all these complexities, it is our intention to use foreign aid for capital development, thus releasing more of our own money for local development."

He showed me a huge "blue book" of agriculture, water, power and transportation projects, prepared by BAPPENAS as a "shopping list" for foreign aid agencies to choose from. It would be much more helpful if the agencies just provided the cash and stayed away from the implementation of the project.

The Afiff position tends to be a bit purist, however. The problem of development in the Third World is caused not just by a shortage of money but the wrong priorities attached to what money there is. The industrialized countries have not forced elitist policies on the developing nations. Moreover, given the widespread elitism and corruption in countries like Indonesia, the Canadian taxpayer — who thinks he is helping the poor people of the world — has a right to be assured that his money is not being used to buy Cadillacs for Third World government officials.

Verge and I put the question of corruption squarely to Dr.

Sumiskum, vice-speaker of Indonesia's House of Assembly. A life-size portrait of President Suharto hovered over us as we gathered around an ornate teak table in his office. A man noted for his outspokenness against corruption, he said the government is making no serious effort to stamp it out. Even Opposition Members do not criticize the government for fear of being branded "Communist" or "leftist." One of the root causes of corruption, he said, was the extended family system in which the one who prospers looks after assorted cousins. Therefore, the man with a government job soon finds his expenses exceeding his legitimate income.

For a case history on the effect corruption has on a foreign aid agency, Verge and I drove to the CARE office to see the director Dallas Vipond. CARE receives funds from both CIDA and the Alberta Government. In fact CIDA pressure has been largely responsible for CARE changing its health program from urban-centered hospitals to rural health stations. Vipond estimates that 20% of CARE's $1 million budget is siphoned off by corruption. Bribes for customs officials are, of course, standard but CARE has found the need for additional staff whose sole duties are security, making sure that CARE's medical program is actually delivered to the rural poor. Following fruitless complaints to the Canadian and American embassies, CARE found it necessary to reduce imports to the minimum.

It is very easy for an aid donor to assume a high moral posture on this issue. But I found a lot of sense in a comment made by Vipond's assistant, Meimei Burke, who has several years of work in developing countries behind her despite her youth.

"Sure, a small minority are making money off the suffering of the majority. But how much do you want to help the poor? Corruption is the price you pay to help people. In Indonesia the price is high. It is cheaper in Bangladesh."

No, aid is not a vocation or a business for the soft-hearted or the soft-headed. Aid is by no means a cure for the sins of mankind. In fact, it is itself a reflection of the human greed that has caused such gross maldistribution of the earth's goods.

"The basic question is this," said Peter Johnson, "is it in Canada's interest to operate an aid program? I think it is. We must avoid even more chaos in the world than we now have. If we start hedging our programs because we don't like someone's morality, then everyone's morality becomes questionable."

Indonesia is a spectacular example of development gone astray, a case history of how elitism has victimized millions of people who should by now have broken through the barrier to at least the basic level of human development so apparent in China. Canada's foreign aid has been a willing collaborator in this elitism, despite the efforts of individuals who have known all along that the export of high technology helps the Canadian government's budget more than the Java farmer.

But there is enough change in attitudes taking place to raise a final question as I leave Indonesia. The Indonesian government has learned, finally, that oil, by itself, will not cure rural proverty and is at least giving lip service to the needs of community development. Canada is giving more emphasis to water management programs. Will this slight move to the more human dimensions of development make much of a dent in the armour of big business and self-serving autocrats? Being the ultimate realist, I seize hope wherever I can find it.

December 10:
Bangladesh, the Test Case

I didn't want to go to Bangladesh.

I didn't want to see all this human suffering in what the journalists call the "basket case" of the world.

Bangladesh is a catalogue of woes: constant food shortages and recurrent famines, devastating floods and cyclones, disorder, violence, corruption, an uncontrollable population explosion, failure of government, economic bankruptcy. What hasn't happened to Bangladesh? No wonder the rest of the world views it as a begging bowl.

Of course, I deliberately chose to come here. No country receives as much foreign aid as Bangladesh; 54% of the national budget is financed by foreign grants and credits, and 126 voluntary agencies from around the world are operating here. Like Indonesia, Bangladesh is among Canada's top ten aid recipients. The 1975 World Bank figure of $100 per capita GNP indicates that this is, indeed, the poorest of the major countries. The population of 80 million makes it the eighth largest country in the world. If development can be made to succeed in Bangladesh, it can be made to succeed anywhere.

Even the short history of Bangladesh is as tortuous as the economy. The territory was established in 1947 when the British left India. Pakistan was created as an independent country composed of two wings, West Pakistan, centered on Karachi, and East Pakistan, centered on Dacca. Seventeen hundred kilometres of Indian territory separated the two wings, whose only common bond was their Islamic heritage. The union was never satisfactory; East Pakistan, with the greater population, resented West Pakistan siphoning off Eastern resources. The discontent grew until the Awami League, led by the charismatic figure, Sheikh Mujibur Rahman, declared virtual autonomy in 1971. West Pakistan, led by General Yahya Khan invaded the East, civil war broke out, Sheikh Mujibur was arrested and 10 million East Pakistan refugees fled to safety across the Indian border. It took another invasion by the Indian Army to drive out the West Pakistan troops and on December 16, 1971, East Pakistan, liberated, was re-born as Bangladesh.

Sheikh Mujibur, almost a deity among his people, returned triumphantly to Dacca. But in the next few years adulation turned to anger as it became clear that Mujibur's regime was not only the most disorganized but the most dishonest in Asia. The Awami League bosses turned out to be blackmarket racketeers who hoarded rice during the 1974 famine to drive the price up. The smuggling route to India of food aid became internationally known. The inevitable military putsch murdered Mujibur, and most of his family, in cold blood in 1975. Counter-coups followed and late that year anti-Indian rightist forces emerged, installing a 40-year-old professional soldier, General Ziaur Rahman (known as Zia), at the head of government.   *1975 martial law began*

The stewardess on the Thai Airlines flight from Bangkok to Dacca came by with complimentary champagne on our way to Bangladesh. No thanks, I said. For me, at this moment, it seems important to make a symbolic statement that the developed world has to give up something to help the developing.

I turned to a new book, *Bangladesh: The Test Case of Development* by two World Bank economists Just Faaland and J. R. Parkinson, who set out their argument that it is not too late to reverse the relentless Bengali course to permanent disaster. But the critical question is population. "Bangladesh is the most densely populated country in the world and its position will almost certainly get worse, terribly worse, unless something is done or happens to check the natural increase in population." Nearly 45% of the population are under 15 years of age, and another 40% are in the reproductive age group. The momentum of increase is so powerful that even to hold to a doubling of population by the year 2000, family planning will have to be pushed with a vengeance. Economic growth lags behind population growth now. One can only imagine how much worse conditions will become over the next two decades unless major steps are taken to cut population growth and boost the economy.

Like Indonesia, Bangladesh is a rural country; 93% of the population live in 65 000 small, scattered villages of a few hundred to a thousand people in houses constructed mainly of mud and bamboo. Clean drinking water is scarce, possessions few and the struggle for existence interminable. The Bengali diet consists largely of rice, which is deficient in both calories and protein. Fish and milk are scarce. Only 40% of the population receives sufficient protein. Inadequate nutrition leaves the way open for disease. Child mortality is scandalously high: one-quarter of all children die before their fifth birthday, usually of dysentry or whooping cough, the kind of childhood illnesses that cause little concern in a Western country. Over a third of the work force consists of landless labourers who earn 40¢ for a day's work and are unable to send their children to school. Education is increasing, but 80% of the population is illiterate.

"Nothing short of a continuing massive injection of aid is likely in present circumstances to get the economy off the ground sufficiently quickly to give real impetus to the development effort," Faaland and Parkinson conclude. "It is not easy to see how donor countries can be persuaded to maintain an effort on the scale needed. Bangladesh is not a country of strategic importance to any but her immediate neighbours."

Well over $2 billion in aid has been pumped into Bangladesh since independence in 1971, by the biggest international aid consortium ever assembled. The World Bank has estimated Bangladesh's aid requirements have grown to $1 billion a year.

Canada has provided $240 million since Bangladesh was created, three-quarters of this in food aid. CIDA's budget for 1977–78 was $72.1 million. The major component of the food aid has been wheat and flour. Such commodity items as potash, urea, woodpulp, aluminum, zinc and lead have been sent. The Bangladesh Railway has been helped to improve its equipment and several small power projects have been undertaken. Although some early Canadian aid was in the form of loans, the Canadian government recently cancelled all debt owing by Bangladesh; all aid now is in the form of grants. Perhaps nowhere else are NGO's playing such a central role. The Bangladesh Government gave its highest agricultural award, the Bangobandhu Gold Medal, to the Mennonite Central Committee for achievement in agricultural production. Oxfam-Canada, the Canadian Catholic Organization for Development and Peace and the Canadian Hunger Foundation all have strong local projects.

The heavy concentration on food aid has raised serious questions not only about the loss through corruption and inefficient rationing systems but about the lasting effects of perpetuating dependency on outsiders. Food aid should be considered a relief item; it does not contribute to development and may actually act as a disincentive to farmers. A greater use of fertilizers, high-yielding varieties of seeds and water control are measures that could ensure Bangladesh self-sufficiency in food.

CIDA's president, Paul-Gerin Lajoie, investigated the application of food aid in a recent trip here and he pointed to this dilemma in a graphic way: "During my stay in Bangladesh, I was given the opportunity to visit an orphanage for children whose parents were victims of recent floods. It was one of the most rending experiences of my life. If they survive childhood, these children, who are given two meagre meals per day, will possibly never gain the health and strength to live normal human lives. What I saw . . . raises poignantly the question of the value of our food aid: will it only prolong pain and suffering?" He called for higher Canadian aid priorities for rural development, agriculture, health measures, and family planning. But moving out of food aid means bucking the Treasury Board in Ottawa, for whom food aid has political appeal since it helps to use up the Canadian surplus.

"Looks like a tired city." Ray Verge, beside me, was looking down on the old buildings in the centre of Dacca. The landscape had a gray-brown tone.

I knew I was in for "officialdom" when I saw the group of Canadian and Bengali officials waiting at the gate to meet us. Despite my request given in advance to CIDA in Ottawa that no dinners or receptions be planned for me because they take up too much time, Jack Godsell, then Canadian High Commissioner, produced an itinerary dominated by official functions. It was obvious he had gone to a great amount of trouble for me, but I needed more time for individual meetings to try to get a realistic assessment of the effects of Canadian aid. At a meeting with his three aid officers at the High Commission (the most unpretentious Canadian embassy I have ever seen), I suggested cutting a couple of dinners.

"Can't do," Godsell said, "the invitations are already sent."

"Well, then, let's at least cut this 'working lunch' on the last day," I said. In External Affairs parlance, a "working lunch" is every bit as formal as a non-working lunch. Seldom is anything more memorable uttered than witticisms and half-baked theories. "Let's just have a staff meeting here in my last hour in Dacca," I said.

The itinerary showed that on the overnight rail journey from the port city of Chittagong back to Dacca, I would be travelling in a private car supplied by Bangladesh Railways.

"The only way you will get me into a private railway car is to handle me as a corpse," I said. The very thought of having a whole car for just Verge and me, while hundreds of Bengalis on the same train would be jammed into dirty, third-class cars, sent a shudder up my spine.

"But the railway officials want you to have this car. They'll be offended if you turn it down." Godsell and his first secretary Victor Botari were astonished at my stand. "Besides it's too late to get first-class sleeping reservations."

"Then I'll sit up."

Botari said he would see what he could do.

When Godsell said that he and one of his officers would accompany me on my visits to government officials, I realized that I was being politically smothered. It is standard procedure for the ambassador in the field to accompany government officials from Ottawa when they call on the local government. In Indonesia, Johnson attended my meetings and I found his presence inhibiting — not so much for me as for the local official who knew his words would immediately be bounced up to higher levels.

I asked to speak to Godsell privately.

"I am not a representative of the Canadian government," I told him. "I am here as a Member of Parliament to study the effects of Canadian aid. I appreciate your help in setting up appointments, but I will interview people alone."

Godsell was flabbergasted. What would the Bengali officials think about such a strange departure from protocol?

"It's because I want to find out what they think about Canadian aid programs that I don't want you listening in."

I wondered if I would still be a welcome guest at the bachelor dinner at Godsell's residence, arranged for me to meet Bengali and Canadian officials.

With two hours to spare before the dinner, Verge and I went for a quick tour of Dacca. And I quickly learned a "fact of life" in Bangladesh.

We climbed the steps to the National Mosque, stepping over a sea of beggars of every description, men, women, old, young, whole of body, deformed. Removing our shoes at the door (but carrying them with us) we entered a peaceful, almost elegant interior. Men, alternately prostrated on the floor or reaching out their arms beseechingly to Allah, were making their evening devotions. A Bengali brought us to the centre of the mosque to view the magnificent blue dome from directly underneath.

When we were putting on our shoes at the door, a couple of appealing young boys stuck out their hands in front of me. I gave them a couple of *takas* (a *taka* is worth about 8¢). Immediately we were surrounded by a clamouring group of 50 beggars. Money was in the air and they wanted in on the largesse. If I gave out any more *takas*, a riot might ensue. The only thing to do was to elbow our way quickly through the crowd. I lost Ray and headed for the rows of stalls that lined the square. After wandering for a while, I returned to the car. A few of the more persistent beggars had followed Ray who was now sitting behind locked doors. A man looked at me with haunting eyes as I got in the car. Beside Ray's window was an emaciated women carrying a naked, year-old baby on her hip.

Neither of us could look at the faces anymore.

"We've come to help them, but we turn away from them," I grumbled.

"It's a hard lesson to learn that simple charity, without changing the conditions of their life, is hopeless," Ray said.

We continued on to old Dacca. The crush of people in the twisting streets was almost unbearable. When statisticians talk about density, they really mean human waves, arms pushing against you, dirt underfoot, noise all around. The proprietors of tiny shops, selling jewelry and pots and shirts, sat cross-legged, hawking their goods.

Down by the river the squatter camps, human jungles, gave their distinctive odour, a blend of excrement and cooking food. A "home' consisted of a piece of earth, less then three metres by two metres covered by a framework of bamboo filled in with cardboard and cellophane. In Bangladesh it rains on and off for eight months of the year. All Bengalis seem to have sad eyes, but the expressions here were gaunt. All that can be said about a Dacca slum is that it is hell.

On the way back to the Intercontinental Hotel ($35 a night and payable only in foreign exchange), we drove by the special housing units constructed for the civil service and the military. Some people in Dacca, myself included, wouldn't have to worry about rain tonight.

December 11:
"Live in the Village,
Rebuild the Village"

Today's *Bangladesh Times* carried two front-page stories reflecting the complexity of the development problem in this country. In the first, we learn that the squatter problem in Dacca (the total of about 175 000 is 13% of the city's population) has become acute. The average squatter family, containing six persons, has migrated from depressed rural areas in search of job opportunities, medical care, education and security. The number of squatters greatly exceeds the current capacity of the government's rehabilitation program.

In the second, General Zia, the government head, has called for an increase in Bangladesh exports as the only practical way to minimize the country's dependence on foreign aid. Opening a trade fair at Cox's Bazaar, Zia said that within the past six months Bangladesh had opened trade offices in Beijing, Hong Kong, Nairobi and New York. Jute is the mainstay of Bangladesh's exports, but there is a great potential to earn needed foreign exchange by exporting fish, forestry and finished leather products, as well as handicrafts. Thus, rural development and industrialization are needed at the same time. An editorial notes: "The question of creating a leadership from the people living in the 65 000 villages is central to a concept of village-based national development."

It is apparent that Bangladesh is in a race with time. If poverty and dependence are not to destroy the country, intensive development is necessary. A prerequisite is the replacement of chaos with stability. That is why martial law and Zia's military rule have been accepted by the public. Actually, authoritarian measures have been welcomed by the World Bank and U.S. government, both of whom are a major influence on development policy. Elections have been postponed and opposition parties banned; there are an acknowledged 62 000 political prisoners.

Zia is tough but reputed to be efficient and honest. He had just authorized an increase in the military and police budgets, and the smuggling of donated food out of the country has been stopped. Zia apparently felt secure enough with city-dwellers to raise the price of rice 28% in order to increase the incentive of farmers to grow more.

The World Bank has recommended income distribution in the countryside and heavy investment in agriculture as the first essential steps to development. But industry and power projects still claim the largest portion of the national budget. Only 8% of all credit available through the nationalized banks is lent to farmers. In a nation of 80 million people, there are only 195 000 on the income tax rolls. Even those funds marked for social services are spent on urban based institutions. In short the elitist, top-down development process predominates, although the government seems to be struggling to find a new model.

I spent an hour with the Secretary of the Ministry of Planning, K. Mahmood, who strongly criticized the aid policies of donor countries, including Canada. I did not sense ingratitude in Mahmood, merely a realism that he would have to go on coping with the kind of aid he didn't need. Countries such as Canada are dumping their food surplus into Bangladesh, thus diminishing the incentive to become self-reliant in food production. Of course, Bangladesh was in famine a couple of years ago and needed relief measures. But is it now nearly self-sufficient in food production. It would be more helpful for donor countries to switch to cash which could be spent on creating the facilities for food production, irrigation, farm machinery, fertilizer. As things now stand, Bangladesh has to import $900 million of oil, cement, pharmaceuticals and other manufactured goods. Exports, principally jute, earn only $400 million.

"Therefore, the trade imbalance of $500 million is eroding funds that would otherwise be available for development. Bangladesh is scheduled this year to repay $40 million of its international debt acquired through loans previously received as aid. Our debt service ratio will soon be up to 30%. It takes more and more new aid to pay the debt from the old aid.

"I am afraid the selfish interest of the donor predominates in most aid decisions. Aid ought to enable us to develop our people, not just keep them alive. The donor and the receiver should form a community of common concern. Instead, the situation is as pictured in the cartoon showing the rich people of the world gathered at one end of a boat, pointing at a hole in the other end where the poor people are gathered, and saying, "I'm glad it's not our side that's leaking."

"Can we say that the industrial nations are really trying to help us when they won't buy our jute and, even worse, develop synthetics to make jute obsolete." He pointed to the tan-coloured curtains and rug in his office to show me practical uses for jute.

"Anyone sincerely interested in trying to help us earn more money ourselves would assist us in modernizing the jute industry.

"No, I'm afraid too many people talk about the milk of human kindness but act with the self-interest of the businessman."

Although development can be seen to be inching along, Mahmood said most government planners were now convinced that compulsion would have to be used to limit family size. The provision of health and education services could not keep up with the population explosion. The precise methods of compulsion — vasectomy, late marriages, sterilization — are still being examined.

My next visit was with Dr. M. N. Huda, the country's leading economist, who is a member of the government's Council of Advisors.

"Bangladesh is not a lost cause," he said. "We have been catastrophe-free the past two years. Our agriculture production is up. Our food imports are down. Smuggling is now at the irreducible minimum. The people accept martial law. It is perhaps too soon to say we have made a breakthrough, but I do feel optimistic that our worst years are over. One very positive factor often overlooked is that Bangladesh is a homogeneous country. Everyone speaks Bengali and that makes communication so much easier."

Aid cannot yet be reduced, he added, because the government's development budget is still in a perilous state. Much of the time of officials is spent on coping with the different styles of the donor countries, and he expressed the wish for an enlarged concept of aid as joint ventures rather than handouts. For example, more cohesive planning is needed to set up light industries in rural areas with appropriate technology.

If stability can be maintained, Dr. Huda and his colleagues feel progress can be made on developing the 10 trillion cubic feet of natural gas reserves already discovered. A Harvard University study shows the possibility of producing 50 million tonnes of food grains — against the current production of about 13 million tonnes — if the required fertilizer inputs are made. And all the fertilizer needed can be produced out of Bangladesh's own natural gas reserves. Even oil exploration is underway. The growing sense of self-confidence may diminish the brain drain of engineers and scientists who have been leaving the country in large numbers.

My final call of the morning was on M. Mohsin, a young foreign affairs officer, who is Director General of the East Asia, Pacific and Americas desk. I commented that that was a rather large slice of the world. He agreed, explaining that Bangladesh is so short of trained personnel that the work load has to be doubled up. I found Mohsin a beguiling man who talked, with tears in his eyes, of the terrible hardships suffered by his own family who often saw a rainstorm wipe out a whole crop. He described the scenes of starvation on the streets a few years ago — when rice was at the same time being hoarded or smuggled out of the country.

Then he talked about the present. "We have made a spectacular comeback. There is enough food for two square meals a day. Life is hard but we are not starving." His main problems, he said, lay with India. Bengali insurgents are being trained across the border in India. And India is recalcitrant on the damage she is inflicting on Bangladesh through the Farakka Dam. This is a huge facility through which India is diverting part of the waters of the Ganges from the channel that flows on to Bangladesh, and into the channel that flows toward the Bhagirathi-Hooghly river system to Calcutta and the sea. The purpose of the Farakka is to add enough water to the Hooghly during the dry season to prevent the port of Calcutta from silting up. Contrary to the original agreement, India is now withdrawing water during the dry months with a devastating effect on the agriculture and ecology of one-third of Bangladesh. The dispute is now in the hands of a UN committee.

What it points up is that, properly used, there is enough water for the whole area and, through the massive water-resource projects recommended by the World Bank the agricultural yield of both countries could be dramatically improved.

David Hopper, then president of Canada's International Development Research Centre, has studied the potential of this area of the world. "The plains of northern India, and of Nepal and Bangladesh comprise over 55 million hectares, all of which could be fully irrigated. With present multiple cropping technologies, annual yields of 15 tonnes of food grain per hectare would be commonplace — an aggregate output level that would increase present world grain production by 70%." But unlocking this potential requires development projects and sums of money that dwarf any previous experience with international aid. The northern river plains development might cost between $30 and $50 billion. Is it just a dream? Or could it be made a possibility with some foresight and cooperation? As long as India and Bangladesh battle over the use of the Farakka, enlarged cooperation does not seem likely.

"We need the good will of our immediate neighbours to survive," Mohsin noted. "And out of this stability, perhaps we can plan better for the years ahead."

In the early afternoon Verge and I set out in a land rover for the rural areas, accompanied by Michel Marcouiller, a young Canadian aid officer and Rahat Uddin Ahmed, a 31-year-old Bengali who works for CUSO. The streets of Dacca were crowded with bicycle rickshas. I watched the ricksha-wallahs, as the drivers are called, sweat-soaked as they strained to move their heavy loads. There are about 30 000 drivers in Dacca who pedal their passengers for 5¢ a mile. After paying for the renting of the ricksha, a driver clears about $5 in a good week. Another Dacca sight is large numbers of men, used as draft animals, pulling and pushing great loads on huge two-wheeled carts. It is amazing that such frail-looking bodies can actually move such weights. Along the waterfront we saw hundreds of crafts, laden with cargo, propelled by teams of men with ten-metre-long oars.

Out on Bangladesh's No. 1 Highway, connecting Dacca with Chittagong, we bounced along for three-and-a-half hours on a 100-kilometre trip to Comilla. Three times we had to cross a river by ferry and, as we drove off the last ferry, a jeep containing armed soldiers was waiting to escort us. The route came within three kilometres of the Indian border; apparently the authorities didn't want us kidnapped by local insurgents.

Our first stop was at the Bangladesh Academy for Rural Development, which trains youths to work in villages, promoting economic and social projects to strengthen community life. The movement to agriculture programs and cooperatives in the 400 villages of the Comilla District goes back to the early 1960's. Model programs were set up to enable farmers to organize coops and credit unions to escape the usurious demands of money-lenders. Gradually new seeds, water pumps, insecticides and fertilizers were introduced and training programs started. The traditional community development approach had been to send in an extension worker from the outside, but the academy experimented with training programs for local leaders. The Comilla approach went beyond technical training to a holistic endeavour to transform rural life in general. Education and health projects were integrated into the planning for expanded agriculture production. These small beginnings in rural development were interrupted by the war and a breakdown in administrative supervision. Despite setbacks, however, the soundness of the Comilla approach was evident.

After liberation, renewed organizational efforts led to the Bangladesh Rural Advancement Committee (BRAC) which expanded agricultural and fishing coops to serve a population of 200 000 villagers in northeast Bangladesh. The BRAC program, funded by CUSO and CIDA, embraces public health and family planning as well as improved food production techniques.

The Comilla Academy has become an important training centre, motivating rural youths to dedicate themselves to rural development. Dr. Gupta, the enthusiastic deputy director, told us, "We propagate this idea in the youths: 'Go back to the village, live in the village, rebuild the village, work with the farmers, the village is our Bangladesh and Bangladesh is our village.' "

All of this has led to a new form of Canadian aid in Bangladesh, the CUSO village Technical Training Program, known as Proshika. Pioneered by a CUSO leader, Raymond Courneyer (whose work has been expanded by those he left behind, the ultimate tribute to an aid officer), the program is replacing Canadian volunteers with Bengalis specially trained to extend self-starter development by more and more villagers.

Proshika is based on the premise that the development of any society depends on the development of the men and women in that society. It is wrong to assume that human beings automatically benefit from the export of high technology from a donor country. CUSO, of course, has long known that the bottom up approach is far superior to the top down. But rather than Canadians doing the actual development work, Proshika enables Bengalis to plan and carry out their own community development work. "CUSO's role," Courneyer has written, "from now on will be very much at the back of the stage, where it should be for a foreign agency working in a developing country."

The man in charge of Proshika is Rahat Uddin Ahmed. He had been quiet during our trip, presumably waiting for me to absorb enough background to appreciate Proshika's advanced role. Rahat has a Master's degree in economics and was recently awarded a scholarship from the Adult Education Department of the University of Massachusetts.

Since village development deals with such practical matters as building poultry and duck farms, fish ponds and improving rice paddy cultivation, Rahat believes in practical education programs. "We have been concerned with involving the villagers in a new kind of learning experience and revealing to them how important they are in making history, and how they could be an element of change and production in their own economy."

I told Rahat I would like to see a village where community development had been introduced. We drove for several kilometres along the highway and then got out of the land rover. There wasn't a sound and I couldn't see a thing. "Follow me," Rahat said, setting off on a trail through the forest. The trail wound around trees and rocks for 300 metres and suddenly I found myself in a cluster of mud huts. The village of North Rampur.

Some 30 men gathered around Rahat whom they clearly regarded as a friend and counsellor. They took us to their "clubhouse," a thatched-roof hut five by six metres, lit by a single bulb. We sat on wooden benches as the men related how, as landless peasants, they were bankrupt, disorganized and despondent before Rahat came to the village.

Rahat had made them realize they must work together and help themselves. They began vaccinating cattle, raising chickens, stocking two fish tanks, all the while depositing their small profits in a credit union. In a year they had accumulated $1800 which was used to enable three landless farmers to buy a little land. They established a rule that even when the money was paid back the beneficiaries had to maintain regular deposits to build up the credit union. With a $250 loan from CUSO, the club bought ten cows, later selling them for a 100% profit. A special fund was opened to buy rice for the poorest among them. The women began to save a handful of rice a day as their contribution to the joint savings. In two months they saved $14 this way and intend to use the money to buy goats.

After these accomplishments had been detailed, Idras Mia, a village elder with a long white beard, spoke up, "At last we're free from the pressure of money-lenders. I have more hope for the young when I see the people here working together now."

The group is currently negotiating with a local land owner to obtain one acre of land for each member of the cooperative. The men plan to work this land together on the basis of one-third of the proceeds going to the landlord and two-thirds to them. The usual arrangement in Bangladesh is one-half for the land owner and one-half for the tenant.

Most of Canada's high technology aid projects are in the millions of dollars. CIDA has put an initial $75 000 into the Proshika program. At last I was seeing the results of pennies well spent. The sums sounded ridiculously small. Yet as I looked into the faces of the men and saw their pride and hope — that I had certainly not seen in the slums of Dacca — the full implications of helping individuals determine and develop their own growth struck home. The villagers of North Rampur had grasped hold of the development process.

As we left the village, a boy walked beside me holding a lantern by my feet so I would not trip on the rocky trail. Overhead the stars shone brilliantly. I realized that I had just experienced the most intimate aspects of development. Suddenly I felt better about Bangladesh.

"The thing that thrilled me most," Ray said, "was the way they said, 'We did this' and 'We did that,' and not "Somebody gave us.' "

When we returned to the land rover, a messenger from another village was waiting with an invitation to visit. A kilometre or so down the road we parked again, stumbled through rice paddies and assembled with the members of another of Rahat's clubs. About 15 young men with a total of $6 formed a cooperative, bought fish to stock in an unused ditch, and later sold the fish for a profit. They started a common vegetable garden and with the profits enlarged the garden and started a new fish pond.

We asked one man, who has a two-year-old child, what the coop meant in his own life. "I know I am better off," he replied. "I have $14 in my savings account. I do not deal with money-lenders any more. I feel more secure."

Again one of the respected leaders told us he would never have believed it possible to see such leadership develop in his own village.

There is no doubt that when cooperatives work well they activate the community, giving it a sense of common purpose. But where management committees break down, as they frequently do, the development process suffers. Trained leaders are essential. As the cooperative becomes the centre of the village activities, it is the sole supplier of inputs of fertilizer and seed as well as the marketing agency, it is the means through which decisions are taken about what crops to plant, it assumes responsibility for the purchase of consumer goods.

In short, advanced coops test communal will and common purposes. When local government is not prepared to deal with villagers with a collective plan and when the local elite (the top 10% of land owners in the country own 34% of the land) react against the incursions on their monopolistic privileges — then community development hits firm roadblocks. Patience, persistence and skills are needed in rural development. It does not come easily. Without a strong push by the central government and the willing cooperation of donor countries in financing this development without getting in the way of it, rural development will be slow. Rahat and his colleagues will continue their work but they need much more support.

December 12:
The Mennonites are Effective

Now I can add motorcycle to the list of vehicles that have conveyed me during this trip. Gerhard Neufeld, a poultry specialist from Manitoba, is one of the 29 agriculturalists with the Mennonite Central Committee (MCC) working in Bangladesh. His Honda XL100 is his means of transportation as he dashes through the Noakhali District (pop. 3 million), watching over the 800 hectares of vegetables, potatoes, wheat, soybeans, sorghum and sunflowers MCC has pioneered as winter crops. Helmet firmly attached, I rode on the rear seat through villages where the pattern of feudal life seems never to have changed.

Ray Verge and I spent most of today with the MCC group, a vigorous band of Canadians and Americans sent overseas by the Mennonite Churches of North America. MCC works in 30 countries and has been in Bangladesh for four years, pursuing a program to help Bengalis attain nutritional self-sufficiency through cultivating land that has traditionally lain fallow during the dry winter season.

The MCC discipline and skill make it one of the most effective NGO's. If foreigners are still necessary because not enough local leaders have been trained, then MCC is a strong second best. They have an attitude of mediation between the different perspectives brought to development by Westerners and Bengalis. In the stereotyped images each has of the other, the Bengalis seem to us satisfied with traditional ways; we are seen by them always restless to find new ways. They are seen as hostile, suspicious, inferior-feeling; we are seen as dominating and superior. Their devotion is to prayer and ritual; ours to work. They are preoccupied with survival, one day at a time; we are future oriented.

The MCC tries to mediate by studying and using the Bengali language, dialoguing to correct old misunderstandings, witnessing to their own Christian culture while acknowledging Muslim achievements, and sharing technical skills for use in the Asian way. MCC does not proselytize (Christian missionaries found out long ago that Moslems rarely convert). The job is technical help done out of a spirit of loving service. They are, in short, committed, and very well organized, Christians. They are supported by a large Mennonite funding program in their churches at home; CIDA provided an initial $125 000 NGO grant, and by 1981 will have provided $702 500.

Though most MCC volunteers are single, Neufeld has his wife and four-year-old daughter with him. "It's very difficult for a Westerner to be accepted into any kind of village life," he said. "We can't reach either the youth or the women. The best we can do is get the production of vegetables and grain increased to supplement the rice diet. I'd like to see more drive by the people themselves — but I guess that's looking at the situation through Western eyes."

We toured the MCC experimental farm where new seeds and multicropping techniques are tested. MCC operates an extension service in which the agriculturalists fan out through the villages, training farmers and special coordinators.

Irrigation, storage, credit and marketing services are included in the MCC service. So too are programs to expand tubewells. If a group of farmers form a registered coop and agree to grow ten acres of winter wheat and potatoes, MCC will arrange the local financing. MCC imports a 7½ h.p. motor from India, easy to operate, to pump water through a narrow pipe from an average depth of 50 metres.

At one tubewell project we met the local teacher, a 28-year-old man named Himanzshu Bimal Chowdhury, who told us that at least a quarter of his students are malnourished, a condition that holds back their learning. Gathered around us were a dozen ragged children from families not members of the local coop. They said they were hungry and they looked it.

We spotted a couple of "baros" — a collection of huts in the form of a compound. A woman was cooking rice on a fire fueled by a stick of cow dung. The clay floors of the huts had a bit of straw for mattresses. Thin quilts hung out to dry. A baby slept in the sunlight; no one seemed to bother with the flies lighting on the child's face. About 15 people live in this baro, sharing the grain stored in the middle of the compound.

Not far away a farmer was eagerly waiting to show us a splendid garden with a variety of vegetables that had been made possible, he said, by the MCC experts.

December 13:
Satellites, Dysentry, and Food Aid

For the first time in this trip I have had culture shock.

In the early afternoon Verge and I were picked up in Chittagong by Bill Foster, a Canadian electronics engineer who is the technical adviser to Bangladesh's Earth Satellite Station. Built through an $8 million CIDA loan, the station was designed to provide a communication link between East and West Pakistan. The war interrupted the project and only in the past year was it completed to give Bangladesh instant communication with the rest of the world. The High Commissioner's office told me it was the best-known Canadian aid project in the country.

As we climbed the hill tracts north of Chittagong, an army jeep swung behind us. "The local insurgents attacked the power lines in this area a couple of days ago," Foster said. Despite the gradual rise of the land he said it is regularly flooded during the monsoon period and he is forced to do a sort of reverse portage and make part of the daily journey to the station by boat. As we passed through some villages, it was evident that life is even more primitive here than what we saw at Comilla and the MCC district.

A high fence and armed guards surrounded the complex housing a gleaming concoction of panels and dials with bewildering names ("switching mode," "external interlock" "collector overload") providing instant telecommunication to any point on earth. The exotica of the space age lined the walls of the sterile control room.

Foster and a team of Bengali technicians reviewed the wonders of the equipment, all of which had come from Canada. Connected to the INTELSAT (International Telecommunications Satellite

Organization) global system, whose satellites are permanently
parked some 35 700 kilometres in space, the Bangladesh station
permits phone calls to be made around the world and also brings in
television signals. Since there are only 30 000 TV sets in Bangladesh,
global TV is not a priority; the station is used principally to transmit
information between London and Dacca on current trading prices
in commodities. Of 60 channels allocated in the international system to Bangladesh, only 12 are in use.

Foster pushed some buttons and the voice of the INTELSAT op-
erator in Mill Village, Nova Scotia, instantly filled the room.

I was becoming angrier by the minute. The satellite station is
surrounded by a nation of villagers who eke out a daily existence at
the subsistence level — while here is a space-age marvel benefitting
only a fraction of the populace. And this in the name of foreign aid.

That is what put me in culture shock.

Dysentry in the villages because there is no clean water. Magic
buttons in the technological showpiece to bring in a voice from
Mill Village, Nova Scotia.

The top down development model gone mad.

CIDA claims the project would not be approved today as foreign aid. Gerin-Lajoie wants CIDA to concentrate on rural development and agriculture. Nonetheless CIDA is providing half a million
dollars a year to maintain technical servicing of the satellite. That is
more than five times the amount put into Proshika. It is true that
the INTELSAT network will have an important role to play in providing early warning of storm disasters and coordinating relief efforts.
But there is a permanent disaster in the dehumanizing conditions
of life for the millions of villagers that ought to be cleaned up first.

Perhaps the scale of the development problem in Bangladesh
is getting to me. Certainly I'm tired. This morning at a briefing at
the Chittagong Port Authority, which receives all the food donated
by foreign countries, I felt myself falling asleep as the speaker
droned one. The chairman, a product undoubtedly of the British
Colonial Office, insisted on calling me, "Your Excellency."

The main point of interest about the Chittagong port is that it
is too small to handle modern freighters. Consequently, most ships
bearing food are off-loaded, in some cases as far as 80 kilometres
away. The inefficiencies of this system allowed pilferage to get out
of hand. When the *Amoco Cairo* brought a huge shipment of wheat
from Vancouver to Chittagong during the worst period of the famine, a CIDA representative stayed with the food until it was trans-
shipped inland under Bengali guard. Because so much food is
moved through the system by labourers, theft has been easy — if
taking extra grain to feed your family can be called theft. Now, under the Zia administration, security is much stricter.

An automatic grain elevator, which Canada was largely responsible for installing, has a capacity of 100 000 tonnes. The system for transporting food looked efficient. It was clearly under heavy guard.

Despite the satellite spectacle, food is by far the largest component of Canada's aid to Bangladesh. There are many aspects to food aid. It clearly helps the donor country get rid of its surplus. That is acceptable if the receiving country actually needs the food and if it finally gets through to the poorest people. Neither of these conditions obtain in Bangladesh. The country is quickly coming into a surplus position. And the imported food goes mainly into the national food chain where it is sold, not given away, in the markets. This is perfectly legal. Under the agreement with Canada, the Bangladesh government is permitted to sell the food, provided it puts the proceeds into what are called "counterpart funds" to be used for development. These funds become lost in the overall national revenue, and monitoring is almost non-existent. It takes a lot of faith to believe that somehow the diet of a malnourished child in the drylands is enriched by the generosity of the Canadian government.

Even in the record harvest year of 1976, an estimated 360 000 children died of malnutrition. But very little of the 600 000 tonnes of international food (down from the 2.3 million tonnes received during the high famine years) went to the neediest. Only 5% was given away to the destitute — orphans, widows and inhabitants of refugee camps. Another 5% was used to pay about one million unemployed and underemployed rural workers on UN-sponsored food-for-work projects. Fully 90% of international food aid goes into national commercial distribution.

Even Gerin-Lajoie noted, discreetly, the serious weaknesses of the complex ration system, which has "a large bias towards serving the urban areas, which by Bangladesh standards are basically middle class." In general, food is distributed through authorized ration shops to ration card holders. This system provides subsidized food on a priority basis to the military, police and civil servants first, then to the five major urban areas, and finally to the rural areas. In terms of feeding the poor during times of scarcity; or as a mechanism to stabilize price fluctuations, the system is ineffective. It not only creates a budgetary dependance but induces complacency on the whole food problem.

Food aid on a continuing basis is counter-productive since it reduces pressure on the recipient government to invest in agriculture. The current Bangladesh budget allocates only 13% of government resources to agriculture. Investment in industry over agriculture is clearly favoured. Farmers have great difficulty getting bank credit. Since the inroads made by the cooperative movement are still small, most peasants rely on local lenders and their landlords for agricultural credit. As a result, indentured labour is widespread and farmers do not have the resources to invest in fertilisers, hand pumps, and the new high-yield seeds. Food aid thus acts as a disincentive; without it, the government would have to pursue a vigorous domestic grain procurement policy. There is such a strong political push by donor countries to continue food aid (the threat of impending famines related to skyrocketing populations is a well-used legislative argument) that it is unlikely an aid switch from crops to cash will be made soon.

Kai Bird and Susan Goldmark, two development economists from Princeton, investigated what they termed "the food aid conspiracy" in Bangladesh. Their report concluded, "Instead of using the Western world's current largesse strictly on an emergency basis for the destitute and price stabilization to provide incentives for internal production — the Dacca regime is using food to pamper its own politically demanding urban middle class. By not tying food aid to specific development policies geared to increasing domestic food production, the international donors are accomplices to a deadly welfarism."

We went to dinner with a group of priests, sisters and brothers, members of the Holy Cross order, who confirmed from their missionary experience that food aid rarely gets to the malnourished poor in the rural areas. The more ignorant the person, the more subject he or she is to exploitation by local officials who expect their palms to be greased ("buckshee" in local parlance) in return for providing a ration book.

"We often see malnourished mothers in our dispensaries who have never even heard of food aid," said Sister Pauline.

The missionaries, having served in this area for between 15 and 25 years, are innured to local corruption, the slowness of government, and even the lack of understanding of conditions by their religious superiors. They struggle on, providing health and agriculture services, accepting what seems at times impossible situations. Sister Pauline wants to establish a small social service centre for women and girls in her community. The only land available is owned by a Hindu, which means that the Moslem women will never go onto the property. There is space available on church property but religious authorities have turned away from buildings. "We do not need big CIDA projects," she said, "rather aid for small projects that would enable us to reach the people who need our help."

Brother Constantine told of how such a "small project" approach had enabled him to run a model farm for three years to train a dozen extension workers at a total cost of $120 000. CIDA provided one third of this amount, the remainder coming from Oxfam, the Canadian Catholic Organization for Development and Peace and other NGOs. He spoke with as much pride in this project as we had seen earlier in the day when visiting the Lions' Eye Clinic in Chittagong.

A project of Operation Eyesight Universal and the Lion's Club of Canada, the clinic organizes cataract eye operations by the hundreds in the remote areas. An enlargement of the hospital is underway but construction had to be stopped for lack of funds. Blindness and eye diseases are a major affliction in Bangladesh. The hospital has so far handled 10 051 outpatients this year. Medical equipment is sparse. The director, Dr. S. R. Das, is grateful for the combined help he gets from Operation Eyesight and the Lions as well as CIDA and the Alberta government. But he is a man whose pressures arise from recognizing that the need is greater than the resources. On the wall of his office is a plaque: *Service to humanity is the rent we must pay for the space we occupy on this earth.*

All day in Chittagong I have been conscious of space, or the lack of it. As in Dacca, the narrow streets were jammed with rickshas, veiled women carrying babies, men pushing vegetable carts. The blare of music on loudspeakers added to the din. Beggars with outstretched pans were on every corner. One shop sold caskets. A man urinated in a gutter. Two men were washing their bodies at a corner pump. Hawkers were everywhere.

At the train station tonight, the scene was even more depressing. The railway officials were eager to escort us to our sleeping car compartments (Botari had apparently been successful), while Bengalis crowded into dirty wooden benches on the rest of the train, which before morning would have passengers riding on the roof. The divisional manager apologized to Ray for not having a fancy towel. Recently returned from Germany where he had spent two years studying rail maintenance, he said he had spent three hours in a bazaar this afternoon looking for quality towels that he *knew* we would expect.

I went back to the platform for a few minutes before leaving. Dozens of people were curled up in burlap bags on the floor. Others just sat wherever they could find a spot, their eyes pools of sadness as they stared straight ahead. Most of the crowd was transfixed by a black-and-white television set suspended from the ceiling. The program was European with Bengali dubbing. Except for the obvious exploits of a macho detective, I don't know what the plot was. What struck me was the size of the car he drove, the big home he lived in, all the nice furniture, and how beautifully dressed the women were. I looked from the TV into the questioning faces of the Bengalis.

December 14:
The Burden Falls on Women

After the war of liberation in 1971 many widows were left in the villages without the means of earning a livelihood. Women who had been raped by Pakistani or Indian troops were frequently deserted by their husbands. A project was started by the Christian Organization for Relief and Rehabilitation (helped by CIDA and the Alberta government, and the Canadian Catholic Organization of Development and Peace) to market jute handicrafts woven by the women in their homes. Within two years a self-supporting cottage industry had sprung up providing a full-time job for 3 000 women and a supplementary income for another 10 000. The jute coop now operates in 16 of Bangladesh's 19 districts, sells to the European and North American markets, and has gross sales so far this year of $470 000, which is double last year's figure. The Mennonite Central Committee acts as the local distributor in Canada.

Designers on the staff are exploring new uses for jute. The coop, already a highly successful development project started with a small amount of money, will likely continue to grow. The women have shown an artistry and deftness in making jute into wall hangings, planters, and handbags. In addition to the rates paid for each piece of work, they share a dividend out of the profits.

While we watched the women in the Dacca headquarters testing for quality, a woman arrived with three huge burlap sacks of handicrafts from the women of her village, 200 kilometres away. With her was her three-year-old child. She was agitated because some of the passengers on top of the bus had cut into one of the sacks and stolen some handicrafts.

As the supervisors consoled her, it occurred to me that I had seen little of women in the development process in Bangladesh. The burden of terrible social conditions throughout the country falls mainly on the women. In fact, the women of Bangladesh are one of the most oppressed in the world. But since they are nonvisible and unorganized, their problems are seldom articulated.

From early childhood on, girls are made fully conscious of the feeling that, unlike their brothers who are assets to the family, they are liabilities. They are taught patience and sacrifice in order to accept their inferior status. Whatever is available to the family — food, clothes, health facilities, education — is offered first to the men.

A girl soon learns that a woman's world is her home while the man's world is outside the home. The separation of the two worlds is enforced by the pervasive *purdah* (seclusion) system. From puberty on, a girl's first duty is the tasks at home, cooking, cleaning, serving. Girls do get a bit of education, but the reason is to make them more economically valuable for the marriage that will be arranged. Nearly every girl is married by 19. After her marriage, a girl moves to her husband's household, doing the most menial chores under the supervision of her mother-in-law and even sisters-in-law. The only way she can get security in her husband's household is by producing a male child. The more males she gives birth to, the greater is her security and acceptance. The average rural woman has eleven to twelve pregnancies in the hope of having six or seven surviving children. She has little control over her own body.

Women clean and husk rice, prepare fuel, make sugar and tend the kitchen garden, but their role in the earning of family income is never recognized. They eat only after the males in the family have finished.

Although the streets of the urban centres are crowded few women are seen. They are expected to remain at home. If they do go out in the street, often they are veiled in a heavy black or brown garment, known as a *burqah*, a shapeless garment that covers clothes, head and face. Women in strict *purdah* have a square opening for the face, which is covered by net or occasionally slits. This allows them to breathe and see where they are going. The poorer women at the very least cover their heads in public with their sarees.

Bengali women, writes Dr. Rounaq Jahan, a political scientist at the University of Dacca, in *Women for Women*, "live in a social system which sanctifies an unequal and inferior status for women."

Moving from relief to development projects is at the heart of the Christian Organization for Relief and Rehabilitation (CORR), set up in 1970 to coordinate relief pouring into Bangladesh from Catholic agencies around the world. At first the main job was to provide emergency relief to the survivors of the 1970 cyclone which wrought an incalculable loss of life, crops and livestock. Drinking wells and home ponds were contaminated, roads washed away, and coastal embankments broken down, allowing saline water to pour through agricultural lowlands. Gradually, CORR's director, Father R. W. Timm, an American Holy Cross priest, told us, the agency has been able to start a model farm and agricultural workshops.

This is another complication of life in Bangladesh. While the move from relief to development has a positive tone to it, facilities to cope with disasters will be needed for a long time in Bangladesh. It is one of those crisis-prone areas of the earth where the life-support systems are so thin that the occurrence of relatively minor natural phenomena can cause major disasters with severe adverse human effects. Further, in many poor countries unplanned growth increases those areas' vulnerability to natural disasters. In Bangladesh, for example, population pressures in the delta of the Ganges induce farmers to plow their fields farther and farther out in the tidal lowlands, dangerously near the sea that rose and hurled in upon the delta a few years ago.

The potential for recurrent disaster notwithstanding, the mood in Bangladesh is upbeat, Bernard Zagorin told us. Director of the United Nations Development Program in Bangladesh, Zagarin called a meeting of UN agencies to give Verge and me an overview of the wide-ranging UN programs: agricultural development, fisheries, jute seed production, plant protection, civil aviation, road transport and technical training. The current budget is $18.5 million.

"There's been a substantial change in how Bangladesh is perceived," he said. "It's seen now less as a relief client and more an object of development. Following the cataclysms of the early 1970's, the country has literally had to be put back together. The Bangladesh government is now certainly more development-oriented. We have to accept their priorities. And their priorities for the basics of rural development are getting better."

The UN's Food-for-Work program in Bangladesh has provided seasonal employment for nearly one million workers at 1 100 sites. The program has the virtue of being relief and development at the same time. Workers are paid six pounds of wheat for moving 70 cubic feet of earth per day at construction projects for new dikes, embankments and canals. In fact, the director, Trevor Page, said, "The program is becoming a national movement. More earth has been dug up for canals and embankments than was dug for the

building of the Panama Canal." An international team of economists and agronomists recently evaluated the project and reported
seeing as many as 10 000 people working on the desilting of a 70-
kilometre irrigation canal.

Since Food-for-Work is seen in donor countries to be a positive result of food aid, it is politically popular. And the acclaim it
has received in the world press diminishes the possibility of drop-
ping it, even when its failings are gradually exposed. Father Timm,
in our discussion this morning, expressed concern about the pallia-
tive trap of Food-for-Work.

In times of famine, the program is obviously beneficial. But in
the long run, it contributes to the low sale price of domestic grain
by bringing excess food into the country. "Food-for-Work overlaps
the winter cultivation season," Father Timm said, "and competes
with labour for cultivation of rice and wheat. This tends to drive up
the price of agricultural labour, which makes the Food-for-Work
wage even more unjust. The deficiency of funds for rural development — which makes the Food-for-Work program necessary —
could better be provided through bilateral or UN financial aid."

His observations are the same as those found in other countries using Food-for-Work. Just because it is a better way of distrib-
uting food than outright gifts does not guarantee its soundness. It is
much better to pay people in government-sponsored development
projects and let them use the money to buy local food, increasing
the demand for local food production. The longer donor countries
comfort themselves with the idea that exporting food surplus meets
the world's poverty problem, the harder it will be to build public
support for the structural changes necessary in international monetary and trading systems that will cure the cancer of poverty rather
than just applying more band-aids.

As China becomes more self-sufficient in food and buys less
Canadian wheat, pressure will grow on the Canadian government
to unload the Canadian surplus in Food-for-Work programs. The
farm lobby in Ottawa is a powerful one. Returning from Bangladesh, Gerin-Lajoie told the government, "We will explore a 'work
for food production' program which would use Canadian food aid
as payment to rural workers in their implementation of food production projects." This is the approach of appeasement. Since it is
known that yields could be doubled with improved seeds, fertilizer
and water management, Canadian aid should be focussed on providing the cash to make these gains possible.

That Bangladesh can become and remain self-sufficient in
food production is not in any doubt, according to Dr. Amiral Islam, director of the Bangladesh Rice Research Institute. Partly

funded by CIDA ($400 000 in 1976) and the International Development Research Centre ($418 200), the Institute was founded by the Ford and Rockefeller Foundations to follow up the green revolution. The Institute has its own experimental farm outside Dacca which I drove out to visit.

With ten million hectares in production, Bangladesh is third among the rice growing countries of the world. But yields have never kept up with demand, resulting in the necessity of importing rice. The Institute, designed to spread rice technology among farmers, has so far been able to reach only 15% of the land; but this area last year contributed to 33% of total rice production.

"Technology by itself," Dr. Islam said, "is not a limiting factor in food production. What is limiting is the political will, and hence the money, to apply throughout the land the factors of fertilizer, pesticide, water management, farmer motivation and extension skills." Despite the work of the rice institute, Bangladesh cannot produce significant increases in food production without heavy investments in high yielding varieties of rice, fertilizer, pumps, fuel for irrigation and extensive water control programs, all of which require foreign exchange for both capital and recurring expenditure.

"The transfer of technology," Dr. Islam added, "is also impeded by the land tenure system in which the landlord takes 50% of the yield from the share-cropper. In fact he takes more than that when you count the exhorbitant interest he charges on the money he lends. The small farmer has little incentive to struggle with modern methods if he doesn't see himself improving. That is why the application of technology is a political problem."

The government has begun to break up large land holdings. Twenty-one hectares is now the maximum that can be held by an individual. Though that is a small parcel by North American standards, it is huge in Bangladesh and gives the owner inordinate power over the lives of the landless.

The question about development in Bangladesh now seems to be whether the country can stay on the development path, having found it at last. Today at the Dacca railway yards I met Harold Flynn, a Canadian consulting engineer. "When I first came here a year ago, I was depressed with what I saw," he said. "Now I am very optimistic." He told Verge and me a story that indicates some lessons about aid are finally being learned. To establish a system for repairing Bangladesh's rail equipment, a Canadian firm proposed a new repair plant with the most modern equipment and tools (all made in Canada). The price tag was $30 million. The plan was almost at the acceptance stage when Flynn's firm, Trimac of Calgary, appeared on the scene, proposing instead to convert old sheds into repair shops and produce maintenance manuals in the Bengali language for local workmen to use. The cost: $3 million. When we visited the shop, Bengali workmen waved at us and then turned back to welding a new part onto an old engine.

December 15:
Dr. Zafrullah Chowdhury,
an Angry Man

Dr. Zafrullah Chowdhury took a medical textbook from the shelf and opened it.

"Look at this, there are 1 000 pages on the great diseases of the Western world like heart and cancer, and only 50 pages on diseases of the East. Our doctors know more about thrombosis than scabies or cholera. Is it any wonder they leave the country or stay in the cities?"

Zafrullah Chowdhury, 35, is an angry man. But his anger found a positive outlet in the training of paramedics to work in Bengali villages that have never had health facilities. He is beginning in Bangladesh the equivalent of the Chinese barefoot doctors system. Although his People's Health Centre (*Gonoshasthya Kendra*) at Savar, 40 kilometres north of Dacca, is only four years old, it has already won the Swedish Youth Peace Prize. Dr. Chowdhury has become internationally known. Only three months before my visit he had addressed the IXth International Conference on Health Education in Ottawa.

Although the population of Bangladesh is 93% rural, 75% of the nation's health funds go to urban health care and medical colleges. The rural areas have only one doctor to every 28 000 people. Bengali doctors do not want to go to remote areas not only because the life is difficult but because the equipment they depend on is not available. Even the 205 rural health centres that have been built are conceived of in Western terms: highly-trained staff and beds must be available. "It is not hospital beds in the major centres that are

needed," Dr. Chowdhury said, "but health care in the villages. The
imbalance is absurd. It is the simple diseases like dysentry that kill
the children in the villages."

With the help of Oxfam and Inter Pares, a small Canadian
NGO specializing in aiding Bangladesh, he had opened the health
centre in Savar, the centre of an agricultural community containing
200 000 people in 309 villages, some of which can only be reached
by boat in the summer rains. With a small team of doctors he began training "primary health workers" (paramedics) to go into the
villages and deal with scabies, worms, mild diarrhea, and infections; immunize against smallpox, whooping cough and tuberculo-
sis; raise awareness of hygiene, especially the benefits of clean
water. Paramedics began not only helping the traditional *dais*
(midwives) but giving family planning information. Some have
been trained to do female sterilization. There are now 44 young
men and women from the Savar area working as paramedics (the
training lasts six months to a year). An auxiliary band of volunteers
keep the records and carry out the construction work at the People's Centre.

Another Chowdhury innovation is to charge the villagers
about 10 pennies a month, entitling them to outpatient treatment,
medicines, innoculations, and family planning services. This is the
first health insurance scheme in Bangladesh, and though it is alien
to village tradition it is gradually being accepted. Another tradition
is giving way to progress: female paramedics in uniform ride their
bicycles alone into the villages without jeopardizing their reputa-
tions.

Dr. Chowdhury said that dysentry and scabies had been virtually wiped out in the immediate area. There has not been a smallpox case in the project area, though the World Health Organization
reported cases in bordering counties.

Gonoshasthya Kendra is more than a health project. Its goal is
to raise community standards. Dr. Chowdhury said, "Food, health
and work make a cycle which very often turns into a vicious circle
of poor food, bad health and listless, demoralized work." This holistic approach in which the paramedics come out of the community
itself is far more beneficial, in the Chowdhury view, than the government's program of centralized training which produces skilled
people who have nothing in common with village life. His paramedics are required to spend an hour and a half every morning
working in the fields with the villagers.

To see Dr. Chowdhury's operation at the village level, Verge
and I drove to a field clinic about eight kilometres away. The rutted
trail was almost impassable even with the bucking and heaving

land rover. The clinic, in a small building not much bigger than a house, was recently opened to serve a local population of 6 000. Three paramedics are on duty. A line of mothers with small children were being processed when we arrived. Abdul Based, a 23-year-old paramedic, who is the leader, told us the number coming, about 60 per day, was still light but would increase through word of mouth.

We walked through fields a kilometre or so to one of the villages served by the clinic. The huts were made of a mixture of clay and mud, with grass for a roof. There was no electricity. The nearest water was several hundred metres away. The cooking seemed to be done over small outdoor fires. Long sticks of cow dung were drying. Most of the children were naked and one of them particularly caught my eye, a boy of about eight with the right side of his face blackened. His mother who said her name was Kumu, told us it was a birth injury.

Because we were accompanied by a social worker from the People's Centre, Mrs. Ayesha Aziz, herself a grandmother, the woman invited us into her hut. We sat on plain wood chairs as her eight children gathered around her. Her husband works the land as a sharecropper. There was enough food at the present time, although the children's faces and bellies clearly revealed nutritional deficiencies. The date palm juice, that flows from trees like maple syrup, was very good for them, Kumu said, pointing to the fire outside where a pot of juice was being heated. She did not know how old she was but remembers being married at 13. Her eldest child is 15. Oh yes, the children go to school, she said. That is very important for them.

We circled through the village compound for a little while, talking to some of the elders, sitting in the sun. As we were starting back down the trail Kumu came running after us, carrying a pitcher. She wanted us to have a glass of the warm date palm juice. It was clear that through the date juice, which was all she had to offer, the woman was extending her friendship to these strange, white Westerners who had dropped into her life for a moment. I knew it was a moment I would treasure.

On the way back to the clinic, Abdul, the paramedic, asked me how many children I had. When I said five, he looked at me thoughtfully for a minute. Then he asked, "Haven't you heard of family planning in Canada?"

Our afternoon was spent in the bowels of the jute industry. To say that jute accounts for 85% of Bangladesh's export earnings or that the Adamjee Jute Mills are the largest in the world may sound vague or statistical. When I was finished exploring the meaning of jute I was convinced that Canada could do far more to help Bangladesh get on its feet by forgetting about food aid and buying jute at fair market prices.

Jute begins its life on the fields of Bangladesh where it grows in tall red stalks, looking something like rhubarb. After soaking, golden horse-hair threads are revealed. These fibres are eventually made into twine, sacks and carpet backing, and, as the widows in the Jute Cooperative have shown, into decorative handicrafts. A new use for the stalks has been found in wallboard for housing. When jute is harvested, it is either exported raw or processed at one of the country's 77 jute mills (all administered by the nationalized Bangladesh Jute Mills Corporation). The jute industry, which is at least two centuries old, employs 200 000 workers and provides cash income for several million farm families.

In 1971 Bangladesh accounted for 35% of total world production of raw jute; although India produces a little less, it processes more. In the late 1960's world demand for jute began to slacken because of the development of synthetic substitutes. The war of liberation disrupted the industry. World prices swung wildly. The United Nations Conference on Trade and Development (UNCTAD) began a process to stabilize the prices of jute and other Third World commodities whose prices could not rise as fast as the manufactured goods of the industrialized nations.

Worldwide inflation meant that Bangladesh had to pay more for its imports of oil, fertilizer and cement but could not get the same rising value for its export of jute because jute is not an essential commodity and if the price rises very much it will be totally replaced by synthetics. Taking the year 1972 as a base, by 1976 Bangladesh imports reached an index of 190, while the export price of jute goods rose only to 118. As Mahmood, the Planning Secretary pointed out a few days ago, Bangladesh requires more aid just to cover the worsening foreign exchange imbalance.

The answer to this dilemma lies in Bangladesh exporting more processed jute at higher prices and breaking through the trade barriers that industrialized nations have set up to protect domestic industries. Far from being cooperative, the three major industrial nations in the UNCTAD negotiations (the U.S., West Germany and Japan) are resisting an international jute agreement on the grounds that the need has not been proven. Since the international price of jute declined from 22.6¢ per lb. to 14.3¢ within a six-month period in 1975, it is difficult to accept an argument that the need for stability is not apparent.

Bangladesh and India are proposing that a buffer stock of a million bales of jute be created, which would eliminate fluctuations and shortfalls and lead to greater import earnings for the producing countries. The cost of financing such a buffer stock would be about $60 million, or about 5% of the aid flow into Bangladesh. Despite the heavy flow of aid, there has been very little interest shown in the jute industry and a callous disregard for the trading position of Bangladesh in world markets. Instead of helping, the industrial (consumer) nations have set quotas and tariffs, actively discriminating against jute and jute products.

In Canada, the bulk of our woven jute fabric is imported duty free from India or Bangladesh for carpet backing and sacking, although there is a heavy tariff on finished jute sacks. Price competition with synthetics is the key to sales; and, because synthetics are now widely produced in Europe and the U.S., it is not surprising that almost half the carpet backing imported into Canada is now made of synthetics.

Ian Smillie, executive director of Inter Pares, questions whether it is moral for Canada to encourage jute's competitor, polypropelene, a derivative of natural gas, and thus drive a natural product out of the market. "It makes no sense to respond to the plea of a hungry child while at the same time ignoring the assets, abilities and ambitions of . . . 80 million people," he said in a brief to the Parliamentary Subcommittee on International Development. He is campaigning for the removal of tariffs on jute products and the restricted use of polypropelene by raising the tariff on it and discouraging government support for investment in domestic development. He has proposed that CIDA assist the jute industry by financing a plant to manufacture spare parts for the jute mills. At present most spare parts are imported, which adds $16 million a year to the foreign exchange burden.

The need for a spare parts industry was apparent to us during our tour of Adamjee. The scene could have been the great English sweat shops of the 1800's. Long rows of clanking looms spin, cut and fold the strands of jute on machines that look as if they originated during the industrial revolution. The noise is horrendous and the dust dangerous. It took nearly three hours to walk through the assorted Adamjee mills which employ 25 000 people on two shifts a day. The company has its own living quarters, shops, schools and mosques for the workers.

After a while I just wanted to get out into the fresh air, but the manager insisted that we see the final section where they are trying to make their own spare parts. "This is the section we have to improve," he said, presumably hoping I would pass the word along to CIDA.

Tonight Mahmood gave a small dinner for Verge and me at

the Tung Nan Restaurant. He invited some of his colleagues along
with Godsell and the Canadian aid officers. Offering a toast to Bangladesh, I told Mahmood that I wanted to help his country and
would do so by telling Canadians: first, the Bangladesh government
has taken hold of development; second, the morale of the people is
good; third, Bangladesh needs a revised form of aid from Canada to
enable it to become self-reliant in doing the job of development itself.

December 16: "Tell That to the Canadian People"

Today was the fifth anniversary of the founding of Bangladesh.

A two-hour parade through Dacca, attracting the densest crowds I have ever seen, celebrated the power of the armed forces. Special prayers were offered in the mosques, temples, churches, and viharas for the solidarity and prosperity of the nation. Extra food was served in hospitals, orphanages and child care centres. Cultural and social events were held throughout the country. And, confirming the growing stabilization of the country, the Zia administration released 1 962 political prisoners, bringing the total number released so far to 9 714.

Both the *Bangladesh Times* and the *Bangladesh Observer* published special sections hailing "Victory Day." The role of the military was highlighted with long articles recounting the birth of the Bangladesh Air Force and the heroism of the freedom fighters. The continued development of Bangladesh was an equally strong theme (the plans to develop a tourist industry in Bangladesh reflect an unshakeable Bengali optimism). A Chinese technical team has arrived to explore the possibilities of small irrigation projects. Algeria has assured its help in the search for oil and gas in Bangladesh. General Zia is to inaugurate tomorrow a three-kilometre excavation project along the Brahmaputra River, which will employ 5 000 workers. A photo shows hundreds of people digging a canal in a remote area under the Food-for-Work program. Prominent display is given a report in the *New York Times* that the economy of Bangladesh is in its best shape since independence was won.

Assessing the country's progress, the *Bangladesh Times* notes in an editorial: "We cannot say that we have been able to utilize all the opportunities that the blood and tears of the martyrs have created for us. Where we have failed to choose the right path, where we have faltered to take the right decisions, why the nation was gradually being transformed into a molten mass of inactivity are questions which have been answered by the historic change of late last year and the glorious upsurge of the Armed Forces and the people."

The *Observer* adds: "Over the year or so the people's cooperation with the government has been one of the most remarkable facts of our national life. It is this, indeed, that has made possible marked achievements in the development sector. It has been most marked in the pace of rural development. The self-help philosophy has caught on as a national philosophy, and encouraged in the right spirit, this is capable of giving a good deal more to the nation. By digging canals, constructing embankments, excavating silted rivers, making roads and bridges, the people of Bangladesh have set a great example of self-reliance."

The world image of Bangladesh as a national soup kitchen filled with despondent beggars ought to be finally buried after today's parade. The enthusiasm and vigour of the people filled the air. With some Canadians from the High Commission, Verge and I set out through the crowds to see the parade. By climbing a fence and by scaling a wall by holding onto the drain pipe, we reached the flat roof of a two-storey building. Several hundred Bengalis were there ahead of us but we found a vantage point to watch the stream of floats and bands. Nothing apparently had been spared in gaily decorating the floats to advertise the national development possible through family planning, strengthening village life, Bangladesh Airlines and even the movies playing in Dacca. The marchers moved swiftly, shoulders back and heads high in pride. The morale of the applauding crowd was invigourating.

The core of the parade, of course, were the military units. The armoured vehicles looked old but they were plentiful. There were long columns of soldiers, sailors and airmen. Zia's own regiment, the Bengal Tigers, was wildly cheered.

In establishing a high priority for the military, Bangladesh is no different from most Third World countries. Although the superpowers, Russia and the U.S., and the other major industrial nations are the big spenders in the arms race, which now absorbs more than $350 billion of the world's funds each year, the number of Third World countries with highly sophisticated conventional weapons is growing. The Third World's share of world military expenditure has risen from 5% in 1955 to 17% in 1976. Even more alarming has been the increase in the Third World's share of the international arms trade; about three-quarters of the current global trade in arms is now with the Third World. In fact, military spending of Third World countries in the past decade has increased twice as fast as their economic base and now exceeds the total amount they spend on education and health combined.

"Every gun that is made, every warship launched, every rocket fired, signifies in a final sense a *theft* from those who hunger and are not fed, from those who are cold and are not clothed." It was U.S. President Eisenhower who said this while he was still in the White House. The joining of the disarmament and development problems into a single theme is not a new notion. But it ought to be apparent by now how the arms race is literally stealing from the poor of the world. When countries from all regions and at all stages of development are involved in major and minor arms races, little time and less money can be devoted to improving the lives of ordinary citizens. Barbara Ward, the renowned development specialist, has estimated that the money required for a full program of development of the poor countries over the next *decade* is only one-half the world's *annual* bill for weapons. But beating swords into ploughshares is a challenge of epic proportions, requiring governmental policies of enlightened internationalism that only a new moral view of the world will produce.

From the viewpoint of General Zia, the only way to consolidate the development process in his land of chaos is to rule as a strongman. Law and order are the highest priority. National stability is what makes progress possible. He himself has the reputation of caring about his people. Having seen at first hand the misery of the poorest in the villages, he said in a recent speech that there would never be any real economic development in Bangladesh until the poor are "motivated to help themselves." If he gives rural development at least equal priority with military spending, Zia will have made a major contribution to the development of Bangladesh.

Though the traffic was nearly impassable and the last hours of our stay in Bangladesh closing in, I did not want to leave without visiting Rahat's Proshika training centre. We met a band of 15 young men, all dressed in their *lungis*, who described their preparations for community development work. I presented Rahat with a book on Canada; I liked him and wanted him to know that I would not forget him. Politeness demanded that we stay for cakes, bananas and tea.

Back at the hotel I sent a porter to my room to fetch the baggage while I checked out. I wondered why he was so long. When he

returned he had an old broken shoulder bag that I had discarded
and papers and assorted junk that I had left behind. He asked me to
sign a slip authorizing him to keep what I had discarded. This de-
meaning subservience to the departing Westerner irritated me. But I
signed the slip, realizing that he regarded the procedure as a normal
way to make a few more pennies.

My discussion with the High Commission staff at the summary
meeting left me in a worse mood. Statistics I wanted were back in
Ottawa. The total CIDA support for NGO's was not known. Once
more I was refused the Country Report. I had come to respect the
staff as energetic and dedicated but the lack of information to help
me evaluate Canadian aid — which is the main function of the
High Commission in Bangladesh — was frustrating.

"Look," I said, "I have to justify the use of Canadian funds in
Bangladesh at a time when the Canadian people have serious reservations about the effectiveness of aid."

"Well," responded Jack Godsell, "for Canada to stand by and
do nothing in the face of such enormous need would be a totally
immoral position. We simply cannot take a defeatist position. I
would fight back against anyone who says we shouldn't bother with
aid to Bangladesh. We have done a lot to overcome malnourish-
ment in this country and we should recognize this. It's easy to criticize the earth satellite station but we've learned a lot about development since that decision was made. We're moving ahead on
major rural development programs that will change the lives of millions. Tell that to the Canadian people!"

I told him I was proud of his response and we parted, I think,
friends.

At the airport the porters had their hands out and we had to
offer a little "buckshee" or risk their "forgetting" to put our bags on
the plane.

Finally we were underway. Ray and I were both exhausted,
and I knew the final evaluation of our findings would have to wait
a while. Yet our minds couldn't let go.

We agreed that Ed Laliseng, Rahat and Dr. Chowdhury
should be put before Canadian audiences to tell them what development is all about. For anyone in doubt about the effectiveness of
Canadian aid we would point to the Cikembar development centre,
the jute cooperative, Proshika, Dr. Chowdhury's paramedics, the
eye clinics in Chittagong, and the MCC agriculturalists.

"What I learned most of all," I told Ray, "is that aid and development are two quite different concepts. Most of our money goes
into the tied-aid bilateral process that is of primary benefit to Canada. Only a fraction goes into the community development process

that is of primary benefit to the poorest. Of course, the transportation and communications infrastructure is needed. But the odds will continue to be stacked against true human development in Indonesia and Bangladesh until a higher priority is given health, education and agriculture services."

"You really begin to wonder," Ray said, "if the best form of government in a developing country would be a non-elitist, benevolent, and ruthlessly honest dictatorship with a very strong, simple ideology in which the people could believe."

I told him he was describing China perfectly. Yet I could not accept the totalitarianism of the Chinese regime.

We agreed that Western-style democracy, with its labourious, time-consuming checks and balances, does not meet the crisis in the developing countries brought on by the population, food, energy and capitalization dilemmas. A higher, supra-national form of government seems inevitable, however far off.

"What is essential right now," Ray said, "is to close the gap, not only between the rich and poor nations, but between the few who are rich and the many who are poor within the developing nations. We have to ask ourselves if our insistence on tied aid is closing that gap or making it wider."

"Well," I said, "I think the average Canadian has a humanitarian ethic about all this and just isn't aware that a business ethic forms the basis of government decisions."

Changing ethical frameworks is no easy task. And the villagers of Indonesia and Bangladesh will wait a long time for new imperatives to be felt on the Canadian scene. Meanwhile, significant improvements can be made within the present structures. More monitoring of existing projects to evaluate the human impact. Send less food and buy more jute. Accent water management and rural health projects. Finance the development of indigenous leaders.

Both of us became silent.

Why is it I have more questions than answers about aid — after all I've seen? Why do Canadians know so little about the realities of Asian life despite media technology? Why don't the media portray the creative developments in Asia with the same fervour they report the disasters and conflicts? What is the woman who gave me the date palm juice doing now? What is the woman in Linxian County Seat who welcomed Eva doing now?

If we cut off food aid too abruptly, could it have a disastrous effect in the event of another cyclone? Why did the Bengali officials persist in calling me, "Your Excellency"? Why do Canadian embassies have big cars and big meals? What's right about Canadian aid? And what's wrong? Does Canada really know how to relate to

the Third World? Will I feel guilty about buying Christmas presents
for my family? Why wouldn't I fight to keep my standard of living
that I've worked hard for? How has this trip changed me as an
individual?

I want to think for a while.

Afterword

1979: A New Government. A New Policy?

Now it is two-and-a-half years later.

The new Chinese leadership has consolidated its position in post-Mao China and the era of Modernization has struck with a force that has astonished the world. Though revolutionary rhetoric still sparkles, the attention of the Chinese leaders is rivetted on the common goal of making China a powerful, modern socialist state, in political, economic and military terms, by the year 2000. Deng Xiaoping, senior Vice-Premier and the most prominent man in the regime despite having twice been purged by Mao, summed up the mood, "There must be less empty talk and more hard work." In his closing address to the Eleventh National Congress of the Communist Party of China, he set the direction:

We must grasp revolution, promote production and other work and preparedness against war, and we must exert ourselves and make good the serious losses and the time wasted as a result of sabotage by the 'Gang of Four.' We must face reality, for there are many problems to be tackled and many difficulties to be surmounted. We are convinced that so long as we truly have faith in the masses and rely on them, we can surmount these difficulties one by one and win victory after victory.

That said, Deng rushed into a marriage of pragmatism with ideology. The absorption of "anything good" from foreign countries was blessed in order to speed up the ambitious economic development program. Involving agriculture, industry, science and technology, and national defence, it was, said the *Far Eastern Economic Review*, "a scheme of epic proportions." Wage increases and bonuses for increased production were put into effect for the first time since 1962. Management systems were revamped, even to the extent of borrowing from capitalist economic principles.

Hua Guofeng, who put a spotlight on openness with a trip to the Balkans, unveiled a ten-year economic development program envisaging 120 major industrial projects, including 10 iron and steel complexes, nine non-ferrous metal complexes, eight coal mine projects, 10 oil and gas fields, 30 power stations, six new trunk rail lines and five harbor projects. By 1985, the plan called for a doubling of present steel production to 60 million tonnes and grain output of 400 million tonnes.

To get Western technology into place to make these new targets realistic, the Chinese went on a buying spree in international markets. Capital imports for the first half of 1978 were U.S. $5 billion, compared to $2.78 billion during 1973–77. A long-term trade agreement was signed with Japan, exchanging Chinese crude oil and coal for Japanese technology, plant and construction material. But it was to the technology-rich United States that Deng gave his full attention, barnstorming the country himself in a peak of Sino-U.S. euphoria that culminated in the normalization of relations between the two countries. Big business, in Canada as well as the U.S., drooled at the prospect of a gigantic market of nearly a billion consumers opening up. And there was not enough hotel space in the major cities of China to accommodate the trade missions pouring in.

There is more than business in this new economic friendship. China, fearful of Soviet expansionism (which led to China's border war with Vietnam), sees benefits from a warming association with the U.S. In the Chinese view economic strength, along with ideological purity, is the only guarantee of China's survival. In short, the exigencies of geopolitics have forced China to accelerate economic and technological growth even at the risk of compromising the Maoist model of development.

The first of that model's features to be discarded occurred in higher education. Whereas university and college students were previously selected for their political reliability after service in the fields and factories, it was suddenly decreed that college entrance examinations would be the determining factor. The old policy preserved political purity at the price of intellectual mediocrity. The modernization program demands the development of the best talent possible. Deng coupled this move with a program to send thousands of students abroad for training in advanced technological subjects and languages. In 1979, some 3 000 students will be sent to Western Europe, and 500 to Canada. Do the Chinese authorities feel confident enough in the members of their future intelligensia to let them loose in the West? The modernization momentum demands that the risk be taken. And, of course, young people now know that they can escape being sent to farms and factories after high school by academic excellence which will propel them into higher education.

The pictures in the Western press of Beijing girls disco-dancing have startled many who found the sedateness of China appealing. But no more, for the moment, can be read into this than into the recent comment in the *People's Daily* that "it is necessary to recognize, admit and respect the religious beliefs of the masses"

Much more needs to be known about the full intent of Deng's

modernization. Underneath the surface, wrote Ross Munro, former Toronto *Globe and Mail* Beijing correspondent, lies the most tightly controlled nation on earth. "Today, communism has combined the conformist and anti-individualist tradition of the Chinese past with the techniques and organization of modern totalitarianism to create a unique system for controlling people's lives." He reported that official court proclamations had sentenced individuals to death for such crimes as "intention to distribute counter-revolutionary pamphlets" and "shamelessly supporting the 'Gang of Four,'" and that 200 such executions had taken place since the "moderate" leadership came to power. The Chinese authorities informed Munro, who planned in any event to return to Canada, that his visa would not be renewed, tantamount to expulsion. Munro emphasized the limits to freedom in the new China; Dr. E. H. Johnson, of the Presbyterian Church in Canada, in a letter to the *Globe and Mail*, interpreted the economic and social achievements of China as representing "remarkable moments of hope in Third World development." The very dichotomy that I had left China with.

It is, then, premature to forecast how the movement to modernization will affect the communitarian nature of the country. Rapid technological change always brings profound social problems. And yet, the basic economic and social development of the Chinese — even if they are poor by Western standards — provides a base of human solidity. Unlike the hard-core least developed countries whose 800 million destitute people are the source of United Nations' concern, China has wiped out the destitution and most wretched poverty that had been the lot of the peasantry for three thousand years. Mao's brand of socialism can probably not be replicated elsewhere. Thus it is pointless to talk about China as a model of development. But there is an undoubted lesson to be learned in how Mao promoted mutual cooperation and individual self-denial into national self-reliance. If China is able to maintain even an imperfect egalitarianism in which people throughout the country share in the benefits of technological growth, it will indeed be the country of the twenty-first century. Their experience since Liberation has made the Chinese people conscious, active participants in China's development in an unprecedented manner; they are at least prepared to play an important role in shaping their own economic, social and political future.

* * *

Both Indonesia and Bangladesh held elections since my visit and Suharto and Zia are stronger than ever.

Suharto's Golkar party won 232 of 255 seats in the House of

Representatives with 62% of the vote for a third five-year term; the opposition parties alleged that millions of votes were disallowed on flimsy grounds in East Java, a stronghold of Suharto's opponents.

Visiting Indonesia in 1979, *New York Times* correspondent Henry Kamm reported the country's security system is on the alert to head off even the possibility of an Islamic revolt based on the Iranian example. The similarities in the Iranian and Indonesian situations are striking. Both are large, undeveloped countries that derive most of their revenue from the sale of oil. Like Iran under the Shah, Indonesia is governed by a near absolute ruler considered to be remote from the people and tolerant of widespread corruption by a favoured elite that is believed to flow downward from his family members. Kamm wrote: "University students are dissatisfied with army-administered political restrictions and are painfully aware of a great gap between the rich few and the many poor, and between a capital city marked by conspicuous consumption and an impoverished countryside." World Bank officials in Indonesia, trying to increase the flow of funds to the poor, have conceded that improving the lives of the desperately poor is much more difficult than building roads or dams.

Martial law having stabilized Bangladesh more quickly than expected, Zia felt secure enough to call a national referendum in which 99% of the people voting expressed confidence in him. This was followed by general elections for the 300-member new Parliament, Zia's Nationalist Party capturing a two-thirds majority. Zia arranged for 30 seats to be reserved for women candidates without contest and this apparently succeeded in gaining votes. Despite this progress, an attempted coup d'état by military elements took place, followed by the inevitable executions. A cholera outbreak occurred, most of the victims dying from drinking polluted water.

As if even more evidence were needed about the inadequacies of foreign aid, the Centre for International Policy, a Washington-based research group, released a report showing how aid is siphoned off by large landowners, government officials and the urban middle-class. Two researchers, Betsy Hartmann and James Boyce, who spent nine months living in a bamboo hut in a Bengali village, related how food aid and project aid, which the country depends on, go primarily to those who can afford to pay the market price. Their report argues that foreign aid, so far from helping Bangladesh's poor, is actually perpetuating their plight by allowing the small ruling elite to devote a less than equitable share of the country's resources to rural development, as well as providing a lucrative addition to their personal incomes.

In short, both Indonesia and Bangladesh are continuing the

process of top down development which magnifies the human disparities within each country. The administrations rely for their political security not on building the self-reliance of the nation as a whole but on military forces. Indonesia and Bangladesh are prime examples of the shocking conclusion of the World Bank's World Development Report, 1978: About 40% of the developing world's population, 800 million people, live in absolute poverty, and even projecting optimistic growth rates in the least developed countries; some 600 million people at the end of the century will still remain trapped in absolute poverty.

What we have learned from China is that a human catastrophe of this magnitude can be averted. Basic development can be accomplished in a society when the administration sets the right priorities and motivates people to think and work for the common good. The Chinese have taught us that development depends on a value system. Marxist class struggle has been their route to building the common belief of "serving the people." Our rejection of Marxism, with its severe curtailment of human freedom, should not blind us to the fundamental lesson that development requires the motivation of a society stemming from belief. It is absurd to think that the seeds of human development are found only within Marxism.

But when we look at Indonesia and Bangladesh and other developing countries, we see no system of belief — economic or ideological — that promotes egalitarian social relationships. The developed countries are in no position to impose a system of beliefs, religious or otherwise. That is why foreign aid, construed as the export of our surplus technology, is doomed to fail in promoting true human development. Here in the West many people have stopped believing in technological fixes as the solution to human problems. In fact, it was Western obsession with science as the greatest faith of all that produced the present state of disorder and frustration in so many lives. Other than technology, which is to say the top-down model, the West has no value system to offer Indonesia and Bangladesh. The top-down model does not produce community development.

What I saw verifies a Ford Foundation report, *A Self-reliant Rural Development Policy for the Poor Peasantry of Sonar Bangladesh*:

> Everybody in the (China) village, men and women, ex-rich and poor, staff and peasants, would be working with his own hands. Excavation of tanks, minor irrigation and drainage would be realized in a few years, without any state participation which will be limited to big works. In a Bengali village,

one-third of the population works two-thirds of the time. In a Chinese village two-thirds of the total population works three-thirds of the time: three times more.

The Indonesian and Bengali leaders I talked to identified the bottom-up model with Maoism. Fearing Maoism, they grasp Western technology. The over-all problem of development today is not just the dominance of the industrialized nations; it has also been the fear or inability of Third World leaders to motivate their own people to take development into their own hands.

The Third World is coming to a new appreciation of rural development just at the moment when it is trapped by the spinning wheels of expanding debt caused by aid in the form of loans for Western technology. It cannot be emphasized enough that 90% of the 2 billion people to be born into the world by the year 2000 will be in the poor countries; and the overwhelming percentage of these will be in the rural areas. The most practical way of meeting water, food, shelter and health needs of these people is through solutions peculiar to each locality.

Planners and policy makers in developing countries, seeking to make their largely agrarian economies stronger, more diversified and productive, have mainly stressed the introduction of the latest manufacturing plants and processes. And this is what the industrial nations have mostly wanted to sell or provide in the form of aid. "That is," says David L. Gordon, director of Industrial Development of the World Bank, "what the industrial establishment of these nations has to offer, knows how to produce." But the Western model is not conducive to balanced growth in the poor countries. In virtually all of them, population and labour force are increasing rapidly, good land is scarce, and the redundant workers are pushed into cities where they crowd into squatter settlements and lead a marginal, often almost sub-human existence. The most practical way out of this dilemma in capital-deficit, labour-surplus countries is to foster a wide ranging pattern of small enterprises that would be the natural outgrowth of a concerted plan of community development — at the local level. As the Third Development Decade opens, it is imperative that development strategies — in both the developed and developing countries — focus on the community requirement.

Since my return I have had an unexpected and happy reunion with two of the Asians who had impressed me most on my trip, Ed Laliseng, of Indonesia, and Dr. Zafrullah Chowdhury, of Bangladesh. They were invited to Canada by the Government of Alberta to give lectures. Both the Cikembar village motivator program and the paramedical program are growing, they reported, gently suggesting that Canada is in an instrumental position to stimulate both developed and developing countries to greater concern for more genuine human development.

* * *

In Canada, a new Progressive Conservative government has come to power, and the Canadian International Development Agency now has its own Minister in the Government, Senator Martial Asselin. He takes office at a time when Michel Dupuy, who became CIDA's president in 1977, has tried to effect a tightened management control system. The Auditor General of Canada had criticized "the very unsatisfactory state of financial control" and his audit produced a list of 92 recommendations; Dupuy told three parliamentary committees that he was adequately responding to the Auditor General's criticism. CIDA justifies the addition of 46 employees to its headquarters staff (only 55 of CIDA's staff of 1,060 are in the field) on the grounds of improved internal control. Nonetheless, criticism remains. And media attention given the relatively small number of CIDA "horror stories" has severely damaged CIDA's credibility with parliamentarians. At best, M.P.'s, like their constituents, are skeptical about, if not hostile to, foreign aid. And it is unlikely public confidence in CIDA can be restored without a thorough parliamentary investigation.

When the Liberal government froze CIDA's budget for 1979–80 at the $1.21 billion level of the previous year (thereby lopping off a projected increase of $130 million) there was a general air of approval on Parliament Hill. Actually, CIDA's decreased spending was more than was generally understood, since pressure from the Treasury Board kept CIDA from spending about $100 million in the 1978–79 budget, which then lapsed at the end of the fiscal year.

The new government of Canada has said that there can be no increase in foreign aid, so critical is the financial condition of Canada. Even if the Canadian economic picture improves, a thaw in the foreign aid freeze will be long in coming. The national unity problem and the dramatic effect of a big jump in world oil prices preoccupy national attention. At the very moment when public support is essential to implement any important step in Canadian foreign policy, public support of increased relationships with developing countries is weak.

A real question is whether the UN target of .7% of GNP in Official Development Assistance, the attaining of which has long been a cornerstone of Canadian foreign aid policy, has any real meaning today. Although Sweden, Norway and the Netherlands have all reached the target, the developed countries as a whole are only averaging .31%. Canada, at .45% is declining, and our chief allies, the United Kingdom, at .31%, and the U.S., at .22, are worse still.

When the fifth United Nations Conference on Trade and Development (UNCTAD) opened in Manila in May 1979, UN Secretary General Kurt Waldheim pleaded with the wealthy nations not to let their current economic malaise prevent them from doing more to help the poor nations develop. However, no amount of rhetoric can move the industrialized nations today. High energy prices and the spectre of lengthening lineups at gas stations, world-wide inflation and recession have weakened the political will of the rich nations to be generous. The UN talks about a New International Economic Order. What we have is new disorder with spreading fear as its by-product. The Third World — varying from the oil rich Arab states to the jungle villages of Asia — has such diverse needs and interests that it practically defies being categorized. There is little wonder that a stalemate has developed in North-South relations. It is obvious we are at a turning point, but who knows where we are going?

This is certainly a moment for Canada to analyze what our role in the changing international development scene should be.

It is the thesis of this book that it is good ethics and good economics for Canada to strengthen its relationship with the developing world. It is steadily becoming apparent that it is in the interests of both the developed and developing countries to take practical steps to create a more equal world. Canada should stimulate new development partnerships that would lead not only to more trade but to an improvement in the human condition. Thinking about this subject only in terms of the quantity of foreign aid is so limiting as to be almost irrelevant. It is the quality of our total relationship with the developing world that must now be examined. And, with a new government looking for ways to take innovative, practical steps, just as the Third Development Decade is opening, the time is right.

We should begin by facing the fact that Canada's foreign aid program, despite many excellent individuals and projects, is a failure. Not a failure because of weak administration at home or corruption abroad, not a failure because the impact of world-wide trading systems has superseded aid as a tool of development, but a failure because in the main it does not attempt to produce self-reliant people who can free themselves from economic bondage. There is humanitarian aid sent abroad and there are heroic Canadians working in the developing countries, but these achievements are dwarfed by the magnitude of the CIDA budget that in effect subsidizes Canadian industry.

There is no doubt that a balance sheet of Third World/Canada relations would show that Canada is the net beneficiary of our relationship with the ten largest recipients of Canadian aid.* Our bilateral aid to these ten countries in 1977–78 was $314.7 million, of which $267.5 million was spent in Canada because of the strictures of tied aid. Even though our exports of $429.7 million to these countries in the same period contain goods financed under the aid program, it is clear that the revenue to Canada exceeded our imports of $180.2 million.

Of course, part of Canada's multilateral and NGO aid also flows into the ten countries. Yet this is more than offset by the benefit accruing to Canada from skilled immigration from the least developed countries. This "brain drain" from the developing to the developed countries is called the reverse transfer of technology. The cost of educating the immigrant has been borne by the developing country, yet the benefits of his work go to the adoptive, developed country. An UNCTAD study shows that in the years 1963–72, Canada provided $2.3 billion in Official Development Assistance to the least developed countries; and in that period took in 56 000 skilled immigrants with an imputed capital value of $11.5 billion. The net loss to the developing countries on this item alone was $9.2 billion.

There is still more to the balance sheet. Since the developing countries contain only 7% of all the industry in the world, most of their exports are primary commodities which are systematically undervalued by the consumer (industrial) nations in relation to the increasing prices of manufactured goods which the industrial nations export to the developing. The new wave of protectionism in developed countries further impedes industrialization in the developing. Businessmen across Canada continue to call for more protection through tariffs, quotas and preferential buying to protect Canadian jobs. There were sighs of relief when the long-awaited GATT accord maintained the barriers against textiles, clothing and footwear. The North-South Institute, monitoring the whole field of Canada's role in international development, said the new trade pact (which the developing countries refused to sign) "actually discriminates further against the developing countries by exempting their key manufactured exports from tariff cuts." The Institute warned: "The mounting industrial capability of the Third World cannot be resisted indefinitely, not without stifling hungry new markets for our

---

*Bangladesh, Pakistan, India, Tanzania, Malawi, Sri Lanka, Ghana, Jamaica, Indonesia, Cameroon

exports and perpetuating high-cost, low-productivity industries at home."

Though we say we are helping them, Canada in fact benefits from our relations with the top ten aid recipients. No wonder the President of CIDA told the Empire Club of Toronto to keep supporting foreign aid because 60% of CIDA's budget is spent in Canada for goods and services, creating what he claimed were 100 000 jobs.

CIDA recently signed the largest development grant in its history, $60 million to Tanzania to improve its railway system; 75% of the grant will be spent on Canadian goods and services, including diesel locomotives, telecommunications equipment and consulting services. Upper Volta, one of the most desperately poor societies in the world, received a $40 million grant to help the West African country build secondary roads, improve railways and protect crops; two-thirds of all the materials will come from Canada. Bilateral, high-technology aid, tied to the Canadian economy, continues to dominate CIDA's spending, despite the agency's protestations that it wants to help people in the poorest countries achieve self-reliance.

The continued attempts to justify CIDA on business grounds will prevent CIDA from implementing its own strategy for international development that calls for increased emphasis on rural development of the poorest people. We must understand the paradox of aid: there is little benefit directly to people in developing countries through our emphasis on bilateral tied aid, and there is little direct commercial return to Canada in the development of health, education and marketing services in the villages where the greatest number of the poor live. True aid is an investment in the long-range development of people. If CIDA persists in explaining itself on grounds of immediate commercial return to Canada — when that return is insignificant anyway — it will seriously jeopardize the substantial body of public opinion that supports CIDA on the grounds that it is actually helping the poorest people.

There have been some advances in community development in the past two years, and these should be noted. CIDA shifted $10 million to Canadian Non-Governmental Organizations bringing the NGO total to $50 million in the 1977–78 fiscal year, Dupuy recognizing that the cooperative community development pushed by the NGO's "could have an enormous impact on the lives of millions of people in the Third World." Proshika, the CUSO project to train Bengali leaders, which I visited in Bangladesh, received some good news: its three-year test was so impressive that CIDA increased its funding through a $458 500 bilateral grant for two years. The NGO portion of CIDA's budget is still only 4.2%, however.

Emphasizing quality, rather than quantity, means changing our priorities. The Canadian Hunger Foundation underscored the need for a new attitude when it stated, in a brief to Parliament's Subcommittee on International Development:

> By and large, (CIDA) Bilateral Division's conception and practice of development have been through turn-key projects. In other words, development of the Third World is done in Canada and is transferred, or its transfer is attempted, to the Third World. On the other hand, NGO concepts and practices of development are *that it must occur in the Third World, by the Third World, and under the control of the Third World.*

This returns us to the question of Canada's motivation for a foreign aid program. The government built support for it on humanitarian grounds. It now justifies it because it is good for the Canadian economy. We will not resolve the motivational, and hence operational, conflict until we face up to the terrible complexities of the modern world and integrate our economic and social concerns, both domestic and international.

All of this explains my hesitation in pointing to the .7% international target as the principal measurement of our aid concern. In order to reach it, high-cost technology items would have to be greatly augmented; and I have tried to show that that is not the appropriate aid for the massive numbers of the poorest of the world. Though the NGO sector should definitely receive a greater portion of the CIDA budget, NGO's could not possibly absorb the amounts involved. Multilateral aid could be increased, but not before more is known about the effectiveness of UN agencies in producing self-reliant development. The picture is further complicated by what is now obvious on the international development scene: aid is a small factor in the development budgets of the developing countries themselves. These are the factors that the Clark government must take into account in deciding on a Canadian foreign aid policy for the Third Development Decade of the 1980's.

Despite the contradictions, I believe Canada should continue to support the .7% target. To pull back would be to signal to the world that we are losing our commitment to helping the poorest of the world who are not blessed with the geography, resources, technology and manageable population base of Canada. We would appear to be succumbing to "aid weariness" at the very moment in history when it is possible for the first time, given sufficient political will, for every country to meet the basic needs of its own people. We would be helping Canadians to forget the problems of humanity rather than continuing to stimulate consciences.

The practical course for Canada to follow in maintaining our international credibility is to stick with the target. Increased aid, properly utilized, does give a momentum to development.

There should be no hesitation in restructuring CIDA. As now organized, it is top heavy at headquarters and too thin in the field. With over 2 000 projects in 91 countries, it is trying to do too much. Confusion over its role has a negative effect on public opinion.

In restructuring, the role of commercial promotion should be put under the jurisdiction of Industry, Trade and Commerce, and the financing of enterprises under the Export Development Corporation. These organizations have the expertise to help Canadian businesses develop solid trading relationships in the developing world. I want to emphasize that it is a practical necessity for Canadians to act on the export opportunities presented by Third World markets. In recent years, the Export Development Corporation has greatly increased its public export credits to developing countries. The EDC gives Canada a massive instrument to serve our interests in trade and market development. There is no need to rely on the commercial potential of CIDA, and continuing to do so will lead to further unsatisfactory results in the process of human development.

The North-South Institute holds that, at a time when growing numbers of Third World countries are moving away from dependence on aid and becoming paying customers, "it would be extremely short-sighted for Canada to squander what goodwill it has earned for the sake of a few one-shot sales at subsidized rates." In short, competing for the burgeoning contracts for the expansion of infrastructure services in the Third World would be much healthier for Canadian businessmen than relying on CIDA to get a foot in the door. And, emphasizing the need for private investment in the developing countries, the Canadian government should increase incentives for such investment.

Freed of its present responsibilities to give a high priority to Canadian gains, a leaner CIDA should then concentrate on community development in no more than 30 countries. Released from tied aid provisions, CIDA could do a better job in helping to produce self-reliant people in the developing world. The fostering of better water management, higher agricultural yields, adequate housing, rural health services, widespread education, marketing cooperatives, and credit unions is the proper work of CIDA. This is what basic human needs are all about. The time is right for Canada to insist with the receiving nations that its aid be used this way. But this is more controversial than it appears because many representatives of developing countries fear that basic needs will become a cheap option for the developed countries to direct attention away from the Third World's demands for structural reforms in international systems.

Once we grasp fully that low productivity, in both the developed and developing worlds, is at the heart of present economic instability, it becomes easier to take a systematic approach to Canada's role in world development.

It is in the interest of both rich and poor to boost productivity all over the world, and this can best be done by stabilizing commodity prices, lowering tariff barriers, increasing the flow of capital into the developing world, and improving the transfer of technology. All of this constitutes the North-South dialogue which, unfortunately, has gone astray because it has lost sight of the mutuality of global interests.

The South (the developing countries) wants access to markets at stable and remunerative prices and access to technology, capital and decision-making in order that wealth-producing efforts in the South be expanded. The North (the developed nations), in return, wants access on reasonable terms to energy and other raw materials.

There are important gains to be made by forging a stronger North-South partnership. Most of the industrial countries today are afflicted by high unemployment, slow growth and continuing inflation. Similarly, the developing countries, particularly the poorer ones, suffer directly from the repercussions of this recession — and even those which have gained from the rise in oil prices or exports of manufactures, have lost out from inflation and protectionist pressures in the industrial economies.

To move towards a more dynamic global economy could thus be in the mutual interests of both North and South. By raising the purchasing power among the greatly expanding populations of the South, releasing new resources, and developing new markets for both poor and rich, higher levels of trade can be created within and between all countries. In effect, the developing countries of the South could become one of the engines of resumed progress in the industrial world.

My argument is this: economic growth in the North demands progress in the South.

This idea ought to permeate a new Canadian strategy for international development cooperation in the 1980's. Here is where Canada can play a major bridge-building role in the international community. It is time to assert a moderate yet constructive solution to world poverty that avoids the extremes of utopian solutions and intransigence to structural change. As Maurice J. Williams, chairman of the Development Assistance Committee of OECD, notes, "Broad international support is more likely to be mobilized for evolutionary changes which remove unjust constraints in the international economic order, facilitate an on-going process of structural change, and encourage a concerted effort to help weak and vulnerable people."

The attitude of the new Canadian government will be an important factor in breaking the present North-South impasse. We have no magic button to push, but we can generate a greater momentum in North-South negotiations by declaring that Canada is fully committed to achieving concrete results. Canada is well suited to lead, not be a grudging participant, in the search for new order in the world.

For Canada to achieve a comprehensive and organic approach to development cooperation — a task that it has been failing at — a new start should be made by the government establishing a Canadian Advisory Council on International Development. This body, providing systematic consultations between business, labour and government on such matters as industrial adjustment strategies, would stimulate public support for a renewed development effort in the 1980's.

That renewed effort should lead to the integration of Canada's policies on refugees, immigration, international development and human rights. Human rights are violated by economic and social discrimination as well as political persecution; we should, therefore, adopt an even-handed policy that achieves practical results in our contribution to the alleviation of human suffering throughout the world.

Canada must remain open to people from other countries, but openness is not an answer to the gigantic human problems throughout the world. The plight of refugees cannot be alleviated by bringing them all to Canada any more than expanded emigration is an answer to the Third World poverty.

International development is complex; by its nature it is long-range. But the growing world refugee situation is an immediate need. Could not more of our foreign aid funds be spent on helping refugees today, rather than building highways and bridges that the Third World countries can do for themselves? There are hundreds of Canadians in non-governmental organizations who will go to the refugees, helping them in their developmental needs, if Ottawa would provide the seed money.

Canada's aid strategy proclaims that we want to help the poorest people. But we don't. The poorest — and who is poorer than a refugee? — get the least. In our immigration, we take mainly the best, the very people who can do most to build up the countries they are leaving.

All this provides reason for the integration of our various approaches. There is no one single answer to creating a more humane society in the global community. But we can become more systematic and determined in helping Canada meet its international responsibilities.

Applying these concepts would create a new role and a new image for CIDA. The new government would be making a profound contribution to human betterment and improving economic and social stability which is a basis for peace in the world. To paralyze our thinking about the human condition just because there is a cash crisis would be to lose a new opportunity open to Canada. It is a moment for creative leadership by the Clark government.

*　*　*

Human development is at a turning point in the march of civilization when one age is dying and the new age is not yet born. The old age of narrow nationalisms and ignorance of one another is fading, giving way to the emergence of a new concept of the oneness of mankind. The fantastic advances in science and technology could ensure a life of human dignity for everyone. The Nobel laureate Wassily Leontief, in a United Nations study on "The Future of the World Economy," maintains that in physical terms there are no barriers within the present century to accelerated development of the poor countries. There is proven adequacy for agriculture and mineral development, pollution abatement, investment and industrialization. There has never been a precedent for such a situation in the entire evolution of mankind. We are entering a totally new period of our planet's history. For the first time there is the opportunity to bring about a better life in larger freedom for all the world's people. Through the birth of a sense of world solidarity it is now possible to build a global society of undiminished diversity, self-reliance, security and equity.

Of course this is, at its root, an ethical problem. But to say that does not mean we should merely nod in acquiescence and get back to business. The new age demands a new kind of thinking. And the present atmosphere in Canada, where we are embroiled in the national unity and domestic economic dilemmas, militates against serious thought by politicians, journalists and the public on the issues of stability and equity in the global community. I am not suggesting that a deeper sense of morality will by itself solve the complex problems of human development; but without a new moral view of humanity, conditioned by the new realities of interdependence, we will continue to attempt to cover with band-aids the gaping wounds in the human condition.

When I returned from Asia I went on a speaking tour across

Canada. Night after night I looked into the faces of audiences who were expecting clear, simple answers to my thematic question: the future of Canada and the Third World. I found myself warning audiences not to expect me to wrap up the paradoxes and enigmas of human development into "a nice package with a red ribbon around it." Development is top-down and bottom-up; it is aid and debt and high finance; it has economic, social, political and moral dimensions; it is humanitarian and self-interested; it is Kumu, the woman in the Bangladesh village, and it is myself.

For Further Reading

An Enquiry into the Human Prospect
   R. Heilbroner, W. Norton & Co., New York, 1975.

The Home of Man
   Barbara Ward, McLelland & Stewart, Toronto, 1976.

China as a Model of Development
   Al Imfeld, Orbis Books, Maryknoll, N.Y., 1976.

China: An Introduction for Canadians
   ed. by Ray Wylie, Peter Martin Associates, Toronto, 1973.

Flowers on an Iron Tree
   Ross Terrill, Little, Brown & Co., Boston, 1975.

Families of Fengsheng: Urban Life in China
   Ruth Sidel, Penguin, Markham, Ontario, 1976.

China: Search for Community
   Raymond L. and Rhea M. Whitehead, Friendship Press, New
   York, 1978.

China: The Quality of Life
   Wilfred Burchett, Penguin, Markham, Ontario, 1976.

Bangladesh: The Test Case of Development
   Just Faaland & J. R. Parkinson, C. Hurst & Col., London,
   1976.

Women for Women published for the Women for Women University Study Group, University Press Ltd., Dacca, Bangladesh,
   1975.

The China Difference ed. by Ross Terrill, Harper & Row,
   New York, 1979.

Suggestions for further study

SEARCHING FOR THE REAL CHINA, a study guide for group leaders, by David Ng

CHINA: SEARCH FOR COMMUNITY, by Raymond L. and Rhea M. Whitehead

CHINA LOOK: IDEALS OF LIFE IN POSTER ART

CHINA: TAKE THREE, color filmstrip with cassette and guide

MAP 'N' FACTS: CHINA, map with ink sketches and information

> These materials can be ordered from Friendship Press, 475 Riverside Drive, New York, N.Y. 10027, or from church book stores in Canada

* * *

CHINA AS A MODEL OF DEVELOPMENT, by Al Imfeld, Orbis Books, Maryknoll, N.Y.

LOVE AND STRUGGLE IN MAO'S THOUGHT, by Raymond L. Whitehead, Orbis Books, Maryknoll, N.Y.

WALKING ON TWO LEGS: RURAL DEVELOPMENT IN SOUTH CHINA, by Elizabeth and Graham Johnson, International Development Research Centre, Ottawa, Canada

WITNESS TO JUSTICE: A SOCIETY TO BE TRANSFORMED, Canadian Conference of Catholic Bishops, 90 Parent Avenue, Ottawa, Canada

HOW CHINA FEEDS 800 MILLION PEOPLE, a slide-tape show prepared by the Canada-China Friendship Association, P.O. Box 3304, Halifax South Postal Station, Halifax, Nova Scotia, Canada

HOW THE OTHER HALF DIES, by Susan George, Penguin, London, England

FOOD FIRST, by F. Lappe and J. Collins, Houghton Mifflin, Boston

* * *

The following organizations provide resources for further study:

CANADA CHINA PROGRAMME, CANADIAN COUNCIL OF CHURCHES, 40 St. Clair Avenue East, Toronto, Canada. M4T 1M9 (newsletter: CHINA AND OURSELVES)

CANADIAN CATHOLIC ORGANIZATION FOR DEVELOPMENT AND PEACE, 67 Bond Street, Toronto, Canada. M5B 1X4 (local offices in various regions)

TEN DAYS FOR WORLD DEVELOPMENT, 600 Jarvis Street, Toronto, Canada. M4Y 2J6 (local groups in various regions)

CANADA CHINA FRIENDSHIP ASSOCIATION or CANADIAN CHINA SOCIETY. Organizations exist in most major cities and other centres

K3